GO! FIELD GUIDE
ROCKS AND MINERALS

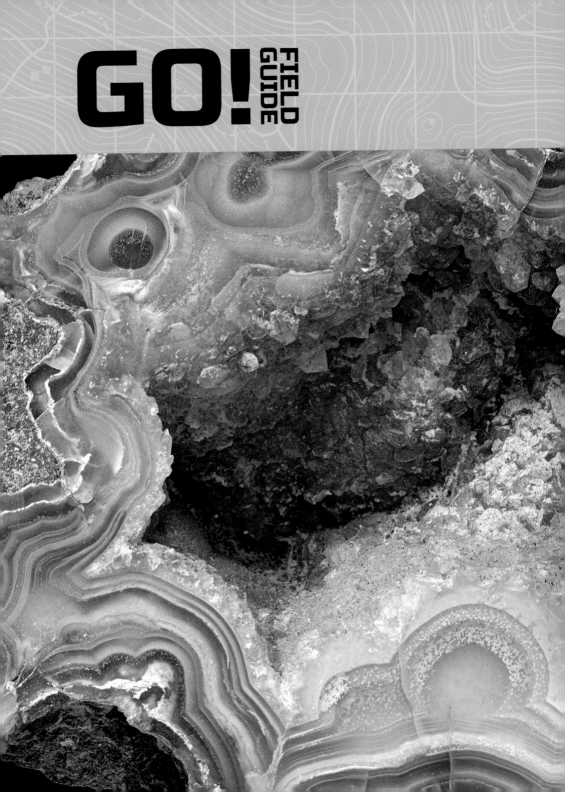

GO! FIELD GUIDE

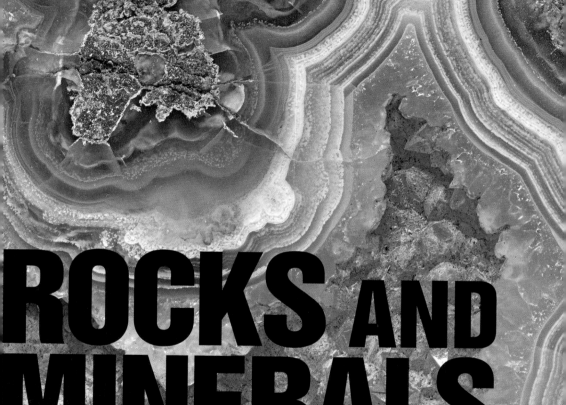

ROCKS AND MINERALS

SCHOLASTIC

New York Toronto London Auckland
Sydney Mexico City New Delhi Hong Kong

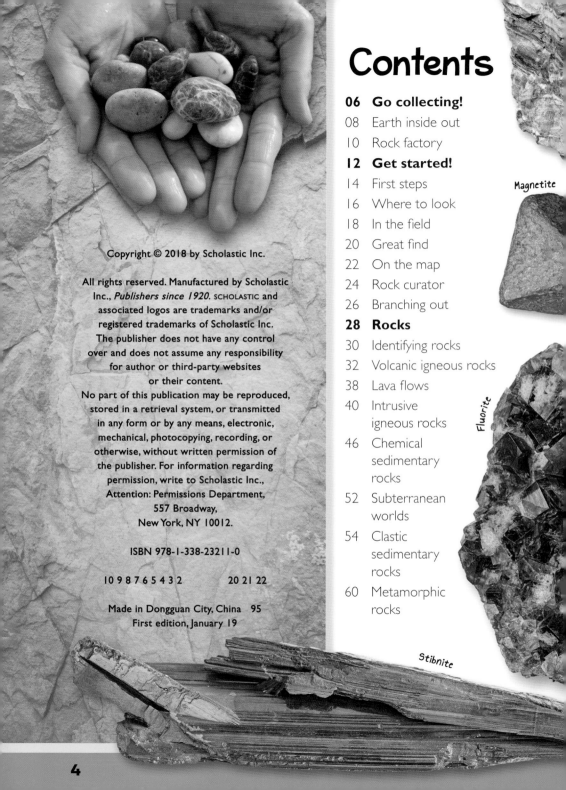

ISBN 978-1-338-23211-0

10 9 8 7 6 5 4 3 2   20 21 22

Made in Dongguan City, China   95
First edition, January 19

Contents

Magnetite

Fluorite

Stibnite

Chert

Diamond

Arsenopyrite

Watch Out! Always
follow the safety advice
where you see this
warning symbol.

Erythrite

Go collecting!

From craggy mountains to pebbly beaches, even in your own backyard, super-cool rocks are everywhere. Get outside and be a rock hound!

Gabbro

Calcite

Gold

Magnetite

Pegmatite

Granite

Chalcedony

Lapis lazuli

Aquamarine cryst.

Silver

Calcite

Nailhead spar

Barite with purple fluorite

Trilobite fossil

Limestone

Tourmaline

Amazonite

Gyrolite

What to collect

Will you collect rocks, minerals, and fossils, or focus on one of the three? You may find fossils on beaches or while examining layers, or beds, of rock.

Rocks are made of minerals. The minerals often take the form of tiny grains. Or they can be crystals that fit together like a jigsaw puzzle. Crystals can vary greatly in size.

Minerals are solid, naturally occurring substances. They are inorganic (not made from living things) and usually made of crystals. A mineral is made of either one chemical element or, more often, several combined.

Fossils are the remains of long-dead plants and animals that have been preserved in stone.

Earth inside out

The ground beneath your feet is Earth's crust and you will find that its rocks are incredible! Earth's interior is made up of rocks that are soft in some places and liquid in others, with a metal center.

The rocky crust is up to 10 times thicker on land than under the oceans.

Planet Earth cutaway

Onion planet

Earth is made up of layers like an onion. Beneath the rigid outer shell, or crust, is the mantle, and below that is the core.

The inner core is a solid ball made of iron with a little nickel.

Tectonic plates

Earth's surface is made up of huge rocky slabs called tectonic plates. The plates float on the softer mantle underneath.

It's hot enough in the upper mantle to soften rock. Some melts into magma, which can erupt from a volcano.

The lower mantle is very hot and super squashed.

The outer core has vast amounts of liquid iron and nickel.

Plates on the move

The plates of Earth's crust are always on the move, sliding over Earth's surface ever so slowly but with incredible force. At some places they collide, at others they pull apart or grind past each other.

Where plates collide, they may crumple up the crust's rock and throw up great mountain ranges. The Himalayas formed where two plates are crunching together.

A rift is a gash in the crust where two plates pull apart. A rift runs all the way through the Atlantic Ocean, deep under water. It can be seen on land at Thingvellir, Iceland.

In some places, two plates slide past one another, such as the San Andreas Fault in California. They may trigger major earthquakes.

A hot spot is a place away from the plate edges where a plume of magma burns through the moving plate above, creating a line of volcanoes. The islands of Hawaii formed in this way.

Rock factory

Over millions of years, water, weather, and Earth's internal heat and pressure slowly destroy old rocks and recycle them. Rocks are organized into three groups that show their stages in this cycle— igneous, sedimentary, and metamorphic.

The rock cycle

Earth has been recycling rocks for billions of years. The minerals you see in rocks today are made from materials that were once part of a different rock.

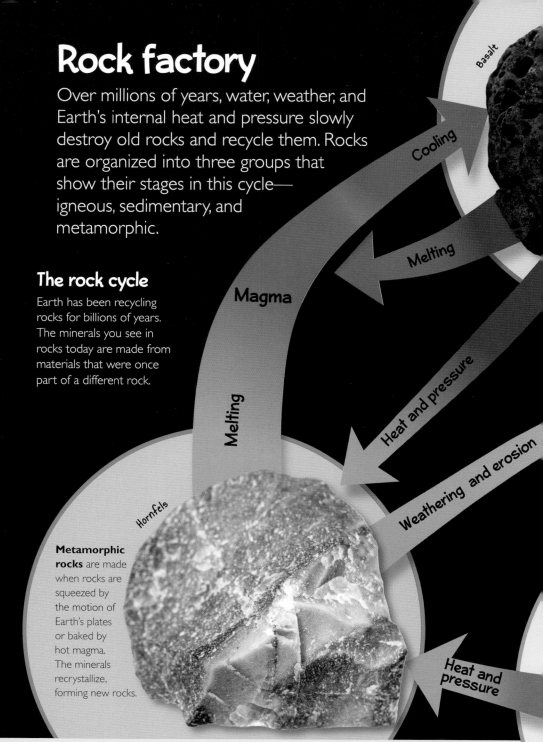

Basalt

Cooling

Melting

Magma

Heat and pressure

Weathering and erosion

Melting

Hornfels

Metamorphic rocks are made when rocks are squeezed by the motion of Earth's plates or baked by hot magma. The minerals recrystallize, forming new rocks.

Heat and pressure

Igneous rocks are created when magma—the molten material of Earth's mantle—solidifies. Some types form when magma cools underground, others after it erupts as lava.

Weathering and erosion

Compaction and cementation

Weathering and erosion

Banded ironstone

Sedimentary rocks are made from sediment— small weathered pieces of rock or organic remains. As the layers of sediment pile up they get compacted (squashed) and then cemented together to form sedimentary rocks.

Weathering and erosion

The rocks at Earth's surface take a beating. They're weathered (changed) by rain, frost, sun, and chemicals in the air. They're also eroded (worn away) by running water, waves, wind, and moving ice.

Repeated frosts can fracture rocks. These rocky spires in Bryce Canyon, Utah, which gets about 200 frosts per year, were formed by frost.

In dry places, windblown sand can carve rocks into weird shapes, such as this "mushroom rock" in the White Desert, Egypt.

Rivers, streams, ocean waves, and moving glacier ice can all wear down rocks. Horseshoe Bend in Arizona was carved out by the Colorado River.

Tree roots can grow down into tiny cracks in rocks. As the roots grow deeper, they gradually force open the cracks and cause the rock to break up.

Get started!

Beachcombing

Beaches are great places to start looking! Here you may find mineral chunks, stones shaped by the waves, and even fossils washed out of cliffs.

Rocks and minerals are all around us, so the adventure can begin the second you step outside. A hike in the hills, a day at the beach, even a stroll in town can kick-start your collection.

First steps

You may not find precious gems, but you don't have to go far to start spotting rocks and minerals in the world all around you. You just need to know how to look.

Home rocks

Even a small garden, backyard, or a local park can contain many more rocks and minerals than you might think. Take a careful look at this picture of some stone steps in a backyard and you'll be amazed.

Limestone boulders

Limestone cement paving stones with igneous rock gravel

Clay bricks

Sandstone boulders

Slate shards

Pink granite gravel

IT'S AMAZING!
Cities can be different colors, depending on the rocks used for building. Paris is famous for its cream-gray Lutetian limestone.

Snapshot!

You don't have to fill your home with rocks to be a rock collector. You just need a camera or smartphone! Take pictures of interesting rocks and keep a virtual collection. Keep a note of the surrounding area to remind yourself where you found them.

The Lutetian limestone of Paris was extracted by tunneling through hillsides nearby.

Rock spotting in the city

Here are some places you might spot rocks just walking down a city street.

- Gravel of basalt, dolerite, or graywacke are often embedded in asphalt to make roads hard-wearing.

- Many buildings contain concrete made from limestone, sand, and gravel.

- Old pavements and patios are often made of flagstone (sedimentary rocks split into slabs).

- Bricks are made from baked clay.

- Sleek modern office buildings may be faced with polished marble.

- Many old houses were built of stone. The famous brownstone houses of New York are made of local sandstone.

- Some older streets were made from granite cobblestones or setts.

Where to look

Some of the best places for rockhounding are also the most fun and the most beautiful. Check out local clubs for great spots near home, and also where you are going on vacation.

Cliffs

At cliffs, rock is exposed by waves and weather. You can find loose chunks that have fallen. But don't get too close! More rocks may fall. And never climb a cliff without an adult.

Riverbeds

In your local river, scoop some gravel with a little water into a shallow pan, then swill out the water. If you're super-lucky, you might find gold or a ruby!

Beaches

Beaches are like superstores for a rock hound. Superb pebbles, already shaped and polished, nestle there—but for the best crystals, look just next to the ocean.

Watch Out! To stay safe when you're out rockhounding, follow the tips on page 23.

Caves

Some caves contain mind-boggling stalactites, stalagmites, and stunning rock and mineral formations. You can visit caves as part of an organized tour.

Hills and mountains

If you're a serious rock hound, try walking in hills and mountains, where the weather exposes the rock and pries out loose specimens. Always go in a group with an adult.

These collectors are hunting fossils in a quarry of Burgess Shale rock in Canada.

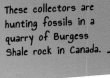

Quarries

In quarries, rock is dug or blasted out of the ground. Working quarries are dangerous places and are strictly off-limits. But some old quarries are open to the public and can be great places to find rock samples.

In the field

Sharp eyes are all you really need to go looking for rocks, minerals, and fossils! A magnifying glass gives you a closer look at grains, and a smartphone helps you record your finds. Then if you want to build a collection, you'll need the basic rock hound's kit.

Smart hounding

A smartphone is your most useful tool. Its GPS tells you exactly where you are. Plus, you can use it to take a photo of every sample you find and the landscape around, with the exact location and time recorded automatically. There are also rock and mineral ID apps you can download to use out in the field.

Getting ready

Dress sensibly for the outdoors and wear sturdy shoes for walking over rocks. A backpack is great for carrying your kit and for stowing away samples, and it leaves your hands free for studying, photographing, and collecting.

Rock-hound kit

Here are the basic items you need:

A magnifying glass with a magnification of 8 times is strong enough to reveal grains—anything stronger will show too small an area.

A hammer is great for breaking up samples. If you can, buy a geological hammer with a tapered point for prying samples apart. A chisel is also handy. Get an adult to help you.

A small trowel helps pry samples from loose ground. Use brushes to get dirt off samples. Roll up your samples in old newspaper or bubble wrap to protect them.

Protect your eyes from splinters by wearing goggles when hammering a rock. Use gloves to protect your hands from sharp edges. Wear a hard hat if you're going hunting near cliffs.

Notebook

Magnifying glass

Geological hammer

Trowel

Toothbrush

Paintbrush

Bubble wrap

Great find

You don't have to be a professional rock hound to find something incredible. In the 1820s, two hikers, Elijah Hamlin and Ezekiel Holmes, discovered tourmaline for the first time in the US. Later, Hamlin's younger brothers, Hannibal (who later served as vice president to Abraham Lincoln) and Cyrus, found more tourmaline nearby.

On the map

Develop your rockhounding know-how by downloading and learning to use geological maps. They help you pin down likely identifications when you're out and about. Once you know where you are going, read the rock rules and away you go!

The rocks beneath

Basic geological maps show "solid geology" —the pattern of solid rocks below the surface. They give you a good picture of what rocks you're likely to see.

Ground slice

Cross sections show a slice down through the ground and reveal how the rock layers lie.

SEDIMENTARY ROCKS
CENOZOIC
Tertiary and Pleistocene
MESOZOIC
Cretaceous
Jurassic
Triassic
PALAEOZOIC
Permian
Carboniferous
Devonian
Silurian
Ordovician
Cambrian
UPPER PROTEROZOIC
Late Precambrian
METAMORPHIC ROCKS
Lower Palaeozoic
Early Precambrian
IGNEOUS ROCKS
Intrusive
Volcanic

ROCK AND ROLL!
Look up local "hounding hot spots" where you can search for specific rocks or minerals that are often found there.

All-important rules

Two simple "dos and don'ts" will make your rock collecting safe and enjoyable. Always go with an adult, or let them know where you are going. Make sure you have permission to collect, as there may be restrictions in some places.

Stay safe! Follow these safety tips to stay safe and enjoy many years of rockhounding.

• Always collect from fallen rocks, rather than trying to remove samples from cliffs or outcrops.

• Only use your hammer for breaking up rocks on the ground. Wear safety gear.

• On a beach, be aware of the local tide times.

• Never climb slopes covered in loose material.

• Don't enter old mines or tunnels.

• Only visit quarries and caves if they are officially open to the public, and go with a guide.

• Never visit cliffs after a storm, when they are more likely to be unstable.

• Only pan in small, shallow streams.

• Always obey warning signs.

• If you're not sure if it's safe—don't go!

Rock curator

Your rock, mineral, and fossil collection starts with the first stone you find. You become the curator of your very own museum—it's your job to clean your items and decide how to record, store, and display them.

Fossil shark teeth

Storage and display

Store specimens in a cool, dry place, spaced apart. You can buy drawers with ready-made compartments, but it's less expensive to make a homemade display, like this, using cardboard trays.

Fossil ammonite

Stalactites

Preparing for storage

Decide how you want to arrange your collection, such as by type, location, color, or alphabetically.

Rock clean up Before storing, brush off loose dirt with an old toothbrush. Only use a hard nailbrush on tough minerals like quartz or hard igneous and metamorphic rocks. You can soak rocks overnight to dislodge stubborn dirt, but before you soak a sample, test it with a drop of water—it might be a soluble mineral!

Specimen No........................
Location...............................
Description...........................
....
Collected by...........Date......

Tagging Always label your specimens carefully. Include details of exactly where and when you found each one, and any identification you have made.

smoky quartz

What to collect You can collect any specimens that look attractive or interesting. Or you may want to concentrate on particular colors or kinds of minerals.

Branching out

If you catch the "rock bug," there are other ways to learn about rocks and minerals and build a collection besides collecting in the field.

Adding to your collection

Hunt for hard-to-find specimens in collectors' stores. Or you can look on the Internet and buy online—with your parents' permission!

Rock shows

Going to shows where rock hounds show off specimens is a great way to see what's out there—and maybe plug a few gaps in your collection.

A professionally sliced and polished agate

Seeing the best

If you want to see the best specimens, go to a museum. They're all clearly identified and labeled. There's no better way to get to know how each mineral looks up close.

Become a geologist

If you're really serious about rockhounding, learn from the professionals. Look up clubs, museums, and universities that organize classes and field trips.

Dig It!
London's Natural History Museum has a collection of more than 123,000 specimens, collected over 250 years.

Polishing

Polished stones make great gifts.

Some minerals look really amazing rounded and polished. You can get this done professionally, or learn to do it yourself with a home tumbler.

Join a club! Find out if you have a rock hounding or geologists' club in your area and find some like-minded rock hounds!

Rocks

Rocks shape the land, build our towns and cities, and inspire us with their spectacular formations. Understand rocks and you'll understand the turbulent, fiery history of planet Earth itself.

Bungle Bungle beehives

The Bungle Bungles are striped, beehive-shaped rock formations in Western Australia. They are composed of layers of sandstone and conglomerate. The dry riverbed in the foreground is made of dolostone.

Identifying rocks

Finding out what a rock is can be tricky. First, you need to figure out whether you have an igneous, sedimentary, or metamorphic rock. Then you can examine the possibilities until you can make a pretty good guess at what you've got.

Where did you find it?

The best clue to a rock's ID? The place you found it. All the rocks in the same area should be fairly similar, so you'll have lots of clues as to whether your rock is igneous, sedimentary, or metamorphic.

The vinegar test

If you have a sample of a white or cream powdery rock, you can try a simple test. Put a few drops of vinegar on the sample. If the vinegar fizzes, there is calcium carbonate in the rock, so it must be limestone, dolomite, or marble.

How does it look and feel?

You can usually tell if a rock is igneous, sedimentary, or metamorphic just by looking at it closely and feeling. See below for what to look for, then pin its ID down more precisely using the charts on page 70–73.

Igneous rocks usually have a hard, shiny, mottled look. With a magnifying glass, you can see they are made from interlocking crystals.

Fine-grained:
- *pale—rhyolite*
- *medium—andesite/trachyte*
- *dark—basalt*

Medium-grained:
- *pale—quartz porphyry*
- *medium—andesite porphyry/monzonite*
- *dark—dolerite*

Coarse-grained:
- *pale—granite*
- *medium—diorite/syenite*
- *dark—gabbro*

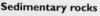

Basalt

Dolerite

Granite

Sedimentary rocks are pale, dull, and even in color. They are made from grains cemented together—the grains rub off if you rub them against another rock.

Dark brown or yellow (clastic rocks)
- *Grains too small to see:* siltstone, claystone, shale, marl, chert
- *Small grains:* sandstone, ironstone, greensand, arkose, graywacke
- *Large grains:* breccia, conglomerate, boulder clay

Pale gray, cream (biochemical rocks)
- *chalk, limestone, dolostone*

Sandstone

Chalk

Breccia

Metamorphic rocks are often more glittery and feel smoother than igneous rocks. If a rock is striped, it is definitely metamorphic.

Banded (striped) rocks
- *Grains too small to see:* slate, phyllite, mylonite, blueschist
- *Visible grains:* schist, biotite mica schist, granulite, gneiss

Non-banded rocks
- *Too soft to scratch glass:* marble, greenstone, serpentinite
- *Hard enough to scratch glass:* hornfels, metaquartzite, eclogite, amphibole

Slate

Hornfels

Volcanic igneous rocks

Magma, molten underground rock, erupts from volcanoes as lava. The lava cools rapidly and mineral crystals form quickly. So, rocks made from lava have fine or no grains.

Legend says the blocks are stepping stones laid by the giant Finn MacCool.

Giant's Causeway

When a mass of basalt lava cools unevenly, it may split into many-sided columns, as seen here at the Giant's Causeway in Antrim, Northern Ireland.

Rock Star!

The ancient Romans used crushed basalt to make roads. And we still use it today!

Basalt

This is a tough, dense rock rich in iron and magnesium. Dark when fresh, it often weathers to green, brown, or gray. It may have holes left by bubbles in the lava and you usually need to use a microscope to see its grains.

TYPE: igneous volcanic
COLOR: dark gray to black
TEXTURE: fine
MAIN MINERALS: plagioclase, pyroxene, olivine
HOW FORMED: above ground, from runny lava flows

Spotlight on basalt

Basalt is the most abundant rock in Earth's crust, forming much of the sea floor. It also occurs on the Moon, Mercury, Venus, and Mars. It's under your feet, too, in the roads and sidewalks of your neighborhood.

The Moon's dark plains, called maria, are basaltic lava flows caused by ancient volcanic eruptions.

Grapes are often grown on basaltic soil near volcanoes. The dark soil is fertile and warms quickly.

Basalt resists weathering better than most rocks, so it is used for road building, as paving blocks, and on train tracks.

The Olmec people of southern Mexico carved huge heads out of basalt around 3,000 years ago. The biggest head stands about 9 ft (2.8 m) tall.

Rhyolite

Rhyolite is a pinkish-brown rock that looks a little like granite. It is made from the same pale, silica-rich magma as granite. But while granite turned to rock underground, rhyolite erupted as lava. It cooled more quickly so its grains are much tinier.

TYPE: volcanic
COLOR: pale pinkish-brown
TEXTURE: fine grained
MAIN MINERALS: quartz, feldspar, mica
HOW FORMED: lava flows, dikes

TYPE: volcanic
COLOR: medium gray or brown
TEXTURE: fine grained
MAIN MINERALS: quartz, feldspar, mica
HOW FORMED: volcanoes at rifts (where plates pull apart) or hot spots (where magama burns through the crust)

Nice Nugget! The word "trachyte" comes from the Greek word

TYPE: volcanic
COLOR: pale pinkish or greenish sand
TEXTURE: fine grained, even glassy
MAIN MINERALS: quartz, feldspar, mica
HOW FORMED: volcanoes, especially lava domes

Dacite

This rock is almost as silica-rich and pale as rhyolite, but it has less quartz and the quartz is in little chunks, or phenocrysts. Dacite is used for road gravel because it is tough yet lightweight.

Trachyte

Fine-grained trachyte is created by the rapid cooling of lava. You can often see tiny white specks of the mineral sanidine in it. Trachyte feels slightly rough because of gas bubbles trapped in the lava.

Quartz porphyry

Porphyries are igneous rocks, containing extra-large crystals, or phenocrysts. In quartz porphyry, quartz and feldspar crystals sit in granite or rhyolite rock like chunks of fat in a raw burger. Ancient quartz porphyries formed in lava flows.

▶▶ **TYPE**: volcanic or hypabyssal intrusive
COLOR: pale red, brown, greenish
TEXTURE: fine grained, with phenocrysts (large crystals)
MAIN MINERALS: quartz, mica
HOW FORMED: lava flows, dikes

LOOK

quartz crystals

white feldspar

"trachys," meaning "rough."

Andesite

Andesites have a "salt and pepper" look, with white feldspar grains (the "salt") set in a dark groundmass of glassy minerals such as mica (the "pepper"). They get their name from the Andes Mountains in South America, where volcanoes erupted.

Dig It!

One of the Mars Rover robots has discovered that andesite is a major component of the Martian crust!

◀◀ **TYPE**: volcanic
COLOR: salt-and-pepper
TEXTURE: fine grained, even glassy
MAIN MINERALS: quartz, feldspar, mica
HOW FORMED: lava, pyroclastic flows (clouds of ash, cinders, and gas)

Tuff

Tuff doesn't live up to its name! It's a soft, porous rock made of ash, dust, and other material that was blasted from a volcano and then compacted after it settled. The fragments that make up tuff are usually a variety of sizes.

▶▶ **TYPE**: igneous volcanic
COLOR: light to dark brown
TEXTURE: fine grained
MAIN MINERALS: volcanic glass fragments
HOW FORMED: from ash, dust, and other volcanic debris

Cracking up!

Q. What do you call a cute volcano?

Ignimbrite

Ignimbrite is a type of tuff that forms when a glowing cloud of ash, cinders, and hot gases, called a pyroclastic flow, rushes from an eruption. When the material settles, the fragments are often welded together by the heat.

▲ **TYPE**: igneous volcanic
COLOR: pale cream, gray, bluish-gray
TEXTURE: fine grained
MAIN MINERALS: volcanic glass fragments, often welded
HOW FORMED: from pyroclastic flows (clouds of ash, cinders, and gas)

Scoria

Scoria is full of hollows formed when lava solidifies around gas bubbles before they escape. It is harder and heavier than pumice and has larger hollows. Scoria may form the top surface of lava flows and build up cinder cones around volcanoes.

▶▶ **TYPE**: igneous volcanic
COLOR: black, dark brown, red
TEXTURE: fine grained
MAIN MINERALS: plagioclase, pyroxene
HOW FORMED: from frothy lava

Rock Star!

Some of today's sharpest knives are obsidian. Stone Age people used obsidian for blades, too!

Pumice

When foamy lava cools quickly, gas bubbles get trapped inside. The result is pumice—a soft, volcanic glass with air pockets, a bit like a rocky sponge.

Dig It!

The best way to find out if you have pumice is to put it in water. It's the only rock that can float.

TYPE: igneous volcanic
COLOR: black, white, yellow, brown
TEXTURE: fine grained
MAIN MINERALS: volcanic glass
HOW FORMED : from frothy lava

Reticulite

Like pumice, reticulite forms from foamy lava. But in this case, the gas bubbles in the lava burst, creating holes rather than air pockets. Although reticulite is lighter than pumice—it's the lightest rock of all—it doesn't float because all its bubbles have burst.

TYPE: igneous volcanic
COLOR: gray, black, golden
TEXTURE: fine grained
MAIN MINERALS: glass
HOW FORMED: from frothy lava

A. Lavable!

Obsidian

This smooth, shiny volcanic glass forms when lava cools so fast that there is no time for crystals to grow. It's usually dark, but after millions of years of slowly absorbing water it goes cloudy. Obsidian breaks into razor-sharp pieces.

TYPE: igneous volcanic
COLOR: black, blue, brown, green, orange, tan, yellow
TEXTURE: glassy
MAIN MINERALS: volcanic glass
HOW FORMED: from silica-rich lava

Pitchstone

Another volcanic glass, pitchstone often has large crystals of minerals such as quartz and plagioclase. It has a higher water content than obsidian, giving it a dull appearance like wax or resin.

TYPE: igneous volcanic
COLOR: black, brown, green red; sometimes mottled or streaked
TEXTURE: glassy
MAIN MINERALS: volcanic glass
HOW FORMED: from silica-rich lava or magma, above or below ground

Lava flows

Red-hot lava from an erupting volcano can flow for hundreds of miles across the landscape, obliterating everything in its path.

The surface of pahoehoe forms a skin of solid rock while the lava continues to flow underneath.

Pahoehoe lava flow, Hawaii

IT'S AMAZING!
Volcanoes can blast lumps of sticky lava, called lava bombs, into the air at up to 1,300 ft (400 m) per second.

The lowdown on lava

The two main types of lava have Hawaiian names: pahoehoe (pronounced "pah-hoey-hoey") and aa ("ah-ah"). A third type, pillow lava, erupts at the bottom of the deep ocean.

Pahoehoe lava moves slowly and develops a smooth or wrinkled skin on top as it flows. It sometimes twists itself into rope-like coils, as shown here.

Aa lava is thicker than pahoehoe and flows too quickly to develop a skin. When cooled, its surface is a mass of jagged lumps that are difficult to walk on safely.

If you're rockhounding on aa lava, be careful of its sharp edges.

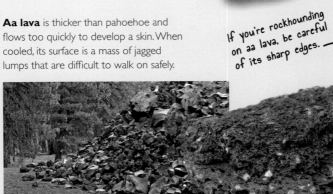

Pillow lava forms where the plates of Earth's crust pull apart on the sea floor. Magma oozes between the plates and quickly cools in the cold water, forming shapes like stony pillows.

Intrusive igneous rocks

These rocks form when magma solidifies underground. Because the magma cools slowly, crystals have time to grow, so these rocks have grains that are varied and easy to see.

Uplifted rock

A batholith is an intrusive igneous rock that has broken above ground. The huge granitic Half Dome in Yosemite National Park, California, was lifted up by mountain building and exposed by weathering.

Half Dome

Tors are granite outcrops in moorland areas left standing long after the surrounding rocks have crumbled away.

Granite

Granite forms deep below the surface. It is a pale, speckled rock with large, visible grains of white or pink feldspar, white or gray quartz, and dark biotite or muscovite mica.

TYPE: plutonic igneous
COLOR: pale pink, brown, or gray with dark specks.
TEXTURE: coarse and granular.
MAIN MINERALS: feldspar, quartz, mica
HOW FORMED: intrusions deep underground

Spotlight on granite

Granite is the most common of all rocks made from magma deep underground—known as plutonic rocks. It is abundant and tough—ideal for making lasting monuments.

The giant presidential heads of South Dakota's Mt. Rushmore are carved out of solid granite on the edge of a batholith.

Granite is incredibly durable. The statues of ancient Egypt still look as new as the day they were carved over 3,000 years ago.

Aberdeen in Scotland is known as the Granite City. The hard-wearing stone resists the city's harsh climate well.

Pink granite gets its color from its high levels of orthoclase feldspar.

White plagioclase feldspar
Black biotite mica
Gray quartz
Pink orthoclase feldspar

Pegmatite

Pegmatites are not a type of rock, but a rock formation. They form when veins and laccoliths (lens-shaped intrusions) cool slowly and solidify around igneous intrusions. Pegmatites often contain huge crystals, which makes them treasure troves for rock hunters. Many gems, such as topaz, can be found in pegmatites.

TYPE: plutonic igneous formation
COLOR: pale pink, whitish
TEXTURE: extra coarse
MAIN MINERALS: quartz, feldspar, and over 500 other minerals
HOW FORMED: laccoliths (lens-shaped intrusions), dikes, veins

Anorthosite

Anorthosites make up the highlands of the Moon, and these rocks were once more abundant on Earth. They still occur in huge formations in Labrador, Canada; and South Africa's Bushveld. Anorthosite is made almost entirely of plagioclase feldspar.

LOOK

labradorite (feldspar) crystals

TYPE: plutonic igneous
COLOR: light gray
TEXTURE: long, streak-like crystals
MAIN MINERALS: plagioclase feldspar
HOW FORMED: large intrusions

Syenite

Syenites got their name because they look similar to granites quarried by the ancient Egyptians at Syene, on the River Nile. They contain less pale quartz than granite and are also slightly less coarse-grained.

TYPE: hypabyssal igneous
COLOR: light pink, gray, white mottled
TEXTURE: coarse to medium
MAIN MINERALS: feldspar, mica, hornblende, pyroxene
HOW FORMED: dikes and other small intrusions

Granodiorite

Granodiorites form in similar places to granite, or even alongside it. This rock contains much less quartz than granite and more plagioclase feldspar and mica. This makes it look darker in color, with a "salt-and-pepper" look. Wyoming's Black Hills contain a great deal of granodiorite.

TYPE: plutonic igneous
COLOR: black and white with pink spots
TEXTURE: even, sometimes porphyritic (a few large grains)
MAIN MINERALS: plagioclase feldspar, quartz, mica
HOW FORMED: intrusions

Dig It!

Most intrusive rocks are pretty tough. If you pick up a speckled pebble on the beach, it's likely to be intrusive.

Diorite

Diorite is basically granite with very little quartz, lots of plagioclase feldspar, and impurities. It often forms in great batholiths with granite along the edges of continents, for example in the Rocky Mountains and Alaska.

> **TYPE**: plutonic igneous
> **COLOR**: speckled black and white
> **TEXTURE**: even, porphyritic (a few large grains)
> **MAIN MINERALS**: plagioclase feldspar, mica, hornblende
> **HOW FORMED**: sills, dikes, batholiths

Peridotite

Peridotite contains a lo of the mineral olivine, s it looks like it's stained with olive oil. It forms in Earth's mantle. In fact, most of the upper mantle is peridotite, but it only rarely comes to the surface.

LOOK

plagioclase feldspar

augite crystals

Gabbro

Gabbro looks like diorite but darker. It forms in giant, saucer-shaped intrusions called lopoliths, such as at Duluth in Minnesota, Rum in Scotland, and the Bushveld in South Africa. The name comes from the village of Gabbro in Tuscany, Italy.

> **TYPE**: plutonic igneous
> **COLOR**: black and white
> **TEXTURE**: very coarse grained
> **MAIN MINERALS**: plagioclase feldspar, mica, hornblende
> **HOW FORMED**: sills and lopoliths (sheet-like intrusions)

Dolerite

TYPE: mantle rock
COLOR: typically dull green to black
TEXTURE: grainy, with small round grains
MAIN MINERALS: wehrlite, olivine, augite
HOW FORMED: interlaid with other rocks and in volcanic pipes

Known as diabase outside of the US, tough dolerite is often used for road making. It is one of the most common sill and dike rocks, and forms New Jersey's Palisades Sill. Identify it by its sugar-grain texture and greenish color.

Rock Star!

About 5,000 years ago, Stone Age people dragged boulders of dolerite to England from Wales to build Stonehenge.

TYPE: hybabyssal intrusive
COLOR: dark, greenish-gray, or black
TEXTURE: medium grained
MAIN MINERALS: feldspar, pyroxene, olivine, mica, magnetite
HOW FORMED: dikes and sills

Kimberlite

Kimberlite forms in sills but especially in narrow, carrot-shaped volcanic vents where hot liquids spew up—often carrying diamonds and garnets with them. The rock is named for Kimberley in South Africa, an area rich in diamonds.

TYPE: intrusive igneous
COLOR: greenish
TEXTURE: medium to coarse grained
MAIN MINERALS: olivine and carbonate minerals
HOW FORMED: volcanic pipes and vents

45

Chemical sedimentary rocks

Some sedimentary rocks form when minerals dissolved in water settle on the seabed. These are chemical sedimentary rocks. Biochemical rocks are made of the remains of living things.

Limestone pavement

Limestone is often broken into blocks by cracks called joints. Rain is slightly acid and it can eat into the joints, which creates flat, grooved landscapes called limestone pavements.

When rain dissolves away limestone, it can create weird landscapes known as karst. The most famous is China's Guilin hills.

Limestone

Limestones are light gray, powdery-looking rocks made from grains of calcium carbonate (calcite). In some limestones, the calcite settled out of the sea. In others, the calcite came from fossils of seashells, and you may see tiny fossils in them.

◀◀ **TYPE**: biochemical sedimentary
COLOR: pale gray
TEXTURE: fine grained
MAIN MINERALS: calcite or aragonite
HOW FORMED: from seashells and dissolved calcite

The blocks are called clints and the grooves are known as grikes.

Spotlight on limestone

There are about 250 million cubic miles (1 billion cubic kilometers) of limestone beds on Earth. All of them are made, ultimately, by sea creatures—which shows just how much life there has been in the oceans!

Limestone is an amazing building material. Millions of Indiana limestone bricks were used in New York's Empire State Building.

The cement used to "glue" buildings together is usually Portland cement. The key ingredient in this mix is is powdered limestone.

Algal and nummulitic limestones are identified by the fossils they contain. **Oolitic** limestone is made of egg-shaped grains of calcite called oolites.

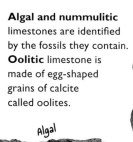

Algal

Oolitic

Nummulitic

47

Chalk

This creamy-white rock is almost pure calcite and so soft you can write with it. Chalk is made from the skeletons of algae (coccoliths) and the shells of single-celled organisms (foraminifera), which lived 100 million years ago (mya).

Rock Star!

Humans first used chalk to create cave paintings over 20,000 years ago. Some can still be seen today.

TYPE: biochemical sedimentary
COLOR: creamy white
TEXTURE: fine grained
MAIN MINERALS: calcite
HOW FORMED: from the remains of algae and sea shells

Dolostone

Dolostone looks a lot like limestone, just a little grayer. But it is at least half made from the mineral dolomite (magnesium carbonate).

TYPE: biochemical sedimentary
COLOR: pale gray
TEXTURE: medium fine grained
MAIN MINERALS: calcite, dolomite
HOW FORMED: from the effect of magnesium-rich sea water on limestone

TYPE: biochemical sedimentary
COLOR: white
TEXTURE: fine, powdery
MAIN MINERALS: silica
HOW FORMED: from diatom skeletons

Diatomite

Diatomite can be very soft and crumbly. It is made from the silica-rich skeletons of microscopic sea creatures called diatoms, which long ago piled up in a sandy slime on the sea floor.

Dig It!

The fossils in biochemical rocks turn them into time machines that give us an amazing picture of ocean life millions of years ago.

Chert

▶▶ **TYPE**: biochemical sedimentary
COLOR: white, gray, black
TEXTURE: glassy
MAIN MINERALS: silica
HOW FORMED: by diagenesis

Chert is not grainy, like other types of sedimentary rock, but almost glassy. It formed when existing sediments were dissolved by chemicals in the ground and then solidified as new sedimentary rock. Chert forms mostly in bumpy chunks or nodules.

When flint is struck against steel, the **spark** can start a **fire.**

Nice Nugget!

Flint

Flint is a kind of chert found as nodules in chalk and limestone. The nodules have a glassy, dark gray interior. Flint breaks into incredibly sharp edges —it was used in the Stone Age for tools and weapons.

▲ **TYPE**: biochemical sedimentary
COLOR: dark gray
TEXTURE: glassy
MAIN MINERALS: silica
HOW FORMED: by diagenesis

Concretions

Concretions are lumps that build up in sedimentary rocks when dissolved minerals dry out around a speck such as a seed, tooth, or bit of fossilized shell. They're typically round and can be as tiny as a grain of sugar or as big as a car. They were once thought to be dinosaur eggs.

▲ **TYPE**: biochemical sedimentary
COLOR: gray
TEXTURE: glassy
MAIN MINERALS: typically calcite or silica
HOW FORMED: from dissolved minerals

Tufa

Evaporite rocks form when mineral-rich waters evaporate, leaving behind solids. Tufas build up around springs like limescale around faucets. Tufas that build up from drips in caves are known as dripstones—stalactites and stalagmites are dripstones.

TYPE: evaporite
COLOR: creamy white
TEXTURE: powdery, spongy
MAIN MINERALS: calcite
HOW FORMED: from lime-rich waters

Travertine

Travertine is like tufa, but tougher, and found only at hot springs. Architects and sculptors often use it instead of marble. Yellowstone National Park is famous for its travertine terraces.

TYPE: evaporite
COLOR: white or honey-colored
TEXTURE: fine grained
MAIN MINERALS: calcite
HOW FORMED: from lime-rich waters

Dig It!

Travertine and tufa are two of the only sedimentary rocks without grains.

Rock gypsum crystals

Rock gypsum

Gypsum can be either a rock or a mineral. As a rock, it is typically found in thick beds or layers. It forms in coastal lagoons where seawater rich in calcium and sulfate evaporates away and is continually topped up with new water.

TYPE: evaporite
COLOR: white
TEXTURE: fine grained
MAIN MINERALS: gypsum
HOW FORMED: in lagoons from sea chemicals

Rock Star!

Gypsum is used in a plaster cast to help fix a broken arm or leg!

Rock salt

Rock salt is rock made mainly of halite, which is the chemical sodium chloride. The salt we use on the dinner table is mainly halite, from thick beds that formed long ago when oceans evaporated in very hot climates.

TYPE: evaporite
COLOR: : white, pink, or red
TEXTURE: crystalline
MAIN MINERALS: halite
HOW FORMED: on the ocean bed

Subterranean worlds

Resembling alien landscapes, the caves and caverns that lurk beneath our feet are full of weird rock formations created over thousands of years by mineral-rich water.

← Stalactite

Dragon Cave, Majorca

← Stalagmite

IT'S AMAZING!
The world's tallest stalagmite, in China, is 230 ft (70 m) high, while the longest stalactite, in Brazil, dangles down 92 ft (28 m).

Mineral sculptures

Water running through limestone dissolves carbonate minerals in the rock. When it trickles into a cave, the water deposits the minerals. Drip by drip, the minerals form standing posts, called stalagmites, and hanging columns like giant icicles, called stalactites.

The rings in this horizontal slice through a rhodochrosite stalactite show that it grew gradually, layer by layer.

Growth rings

Cave bacon is thin, striped sheets that look like bacon slices. Large, curtain-like hanging sheets are called draperies.

Thinner than chunky stalactites, soda straws are delicate long, hollow tubes. They often occur together in large numbers.

Cave pearls are calcite balls found in shallow cave pools. They can be as small as sand grains or as big as golf balls.

Clastic sedimentary rocks

Many sedimentary rocks are made of broken fragments, or clasts, of other rocks. These pile up anywhere, from the seabed to deserts, and are compacted into clastic rock.

Rock waves

The Wave in Arizona is a sandstone formation made from desert sand dunes 190 mya, then carved by the desert wind into fantastic curves.

Sandstone

Sandstones are made in deserts, on riverbeds, or on the seabed. They are formed when sand grains are blown together by the wind or washed together by rivers or waves. Their color comes from whatever material cements the grains, such as reddish iron minerals.

TYPE: clastic sedimentary
COLOR: sandy yellow, brown, red
TEXTURE: sandy
MAIN MINERALS: quartz, feldspar
HOW FORMED: in deserts, on riverbeds and seabeds

Spotlight on sandstone

Igneous rocks have grains locked firmly together, but sedimentary sandstone is friable (crumbly). Quartz grains with a little feldspar are loosely packed with a powder, or matrix, and held together with iron or lime cement.

For thousands of years people have made glass by crumbling out sandstone's quartz grains and washing and melting them.

Sandstone's sharp, tough sand grains make it perfect for making grindstones, used for sharpening knives or milling corn.

Sandstone is easily cut to shape, yet it endures through time. The city of Petra in Jordan was carved out of solid sandstone 2,000 years ago.

Looking closer...

Look closely at the shape of grains— they can give you clues to the rock's origins. The rounder the grains, the farther they've been transported. The most rounded grains form in deserts.

Ironstone

Ironstones are thin layers of rusty-brown sedimentary rock interlayered with clays, sandstones, and limestones. They are over 15 percent iron, but are too rare to be much use as commercial sources of iron.

LÓÓK

red fine- grained texture

Graywacke

The name "graywacke" comes from the German for "gray grit." Like sandstone, graywackes are made mostly from sand, but the sand grains are randomly mixed in with clay, silt, and stones. They formed from the debris of avalanches under the sea.

TYPE: clastic sedimentary
COLOR: red-brown
TEXTURE: fine grained
MAIN MINERALS: quartz, feldspar, and over 15% iron
HOW FORMED: on seabeds near laterites (tropical soils)

Nice Nugget! Uluru, which glows red in Australia's outback,

Orthoquartzite

Orthoquartzites are almost pure silica. Their quartz grains are cemented together by silica rather than iron or lime. These rocks formed from sand that was piled up by waves crashing on a beach. This why the grains are round.

TYPE: clastic sedimentary
COLOR: white, pale gray
TEXTURE: sand-sized grains
MAIN MINERALS: quartz
HOW FORMED: from beach sand

Powdered greensand is used by organic gardeners to improve their soil.

Greensand

Greensand is a sandstone rock tinged green by fine grains of glauconite. Glauconite is a blue-green mineral containing iron and potassium that forms from the chemical change of sediments under the sea.

TYPE: clastic sedimentary
COLOR: greenish gray
TEXTURE: sand-sized grains
MAIN MINERALS: quartz, glauconite, smectite
HOW FORMED: from undersea sediments

TYPE: clastic sedimentary
COLOR: gray, green brown
TEXTURE: mixed
MAIN MINERALS: quartz, feldspar, mica, clay
HOW FORMED: by undersea avalanches

is made of **arkose**.

TYPE: clastic sedimentary
COLOR: gray to red
TEXTURE: medium to coarse grains
MAIN MINERALS: quartz, feldspar
HOW FORMED: from undersea sediments

Arkose

Arkose is a sandstone made of granite fragments. It contains more feldspar and less quartz than other sandstones. Arkose also has larger grains, because it formed quickly in cold or extra-dry places, and is less affected by weathering.

Shale

Shale forms when mud and clay settles on river floodplains and the seabed, then is squeezed into thin layers called laminations. The laminations make the rock look flaky like slate, but it is softer and full of fossils.

TYPE: clastic sedimentary
COLOR: black, gray, white, brown
TEXTURE: super fine grained
MAIN MINERALS: quartz, feldspar, mica
HOW FORMED: from mud on river floodplains and the seabed

Siltstone

Siltstone has slightly coarser grains than shale. It feels gritty and you can actually see the grains. This rock forms closer to the shore than shale—only the finer shale grains are carried farther out.

TYPE: clastic sedimentary
COLOR: pale gray, beige, with bands
TEXTURE: fine
MAIN MINERALS: quartz, feldspar, mica
HOW FORMED: from mud on the seabed and river floodplains

Dig It!

The fine grains of mudstone make it feel smooth and slippery when wet.

Mudstone

Like shale, mudstone's grains are super-fine—so fine you can see them only with a magnifying glass. Unlike shale, it breaks into blocks rather than flat chips.

TYPE: clastic sedimentary
COLOR: black, gray, green, white, red
TEXTURE: super fine grained
MAIN MINERALS: quartz, feldspar, mica
HOW FORMED: from mud on shallow seabeds

In 2012, conglomerate was

LOOK

pebbles or stones in the rock

Marl

Marl is made of the same fine grains as shale. In marl, the silica is mixed with calcium carbonate, or lime, from seashells, giving it a creamy brown color. In the past, marl was added to soil to improve it.

🌲 **TYPE**: clastic sedimentary
COLOR: creamy gray, brown
TEXTURE: super fine grained
MAIN MINERALS: silica, calcite, aragonite
HOW FORMED: from mud on shallow seabeds

Breccia

In most sedimentary rocks, the sediments are sorted as they settle. But breccias are made of piles of unsorted debris from dramatic events such as avalanches. The stones are chunky and sharp-cornered.

🌲 **TYPE**: clastic sedimentary
COLOR: varied
TEXTURE: very mixed, with some big stones
MAIN MINERALS: variable, but lots of quartz
HOW FORMED: by avalanches

...und on **Mars**, proving Mars once had **water on it!**

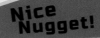

Nice Nugget!

Conglomerate

Like breccia, conglomerates are made from chaotic mixtures of stones. The stones in conglomerates are piled up by fast-flowing rivers, and you can see how they have been smoothed into pebbles by the running water.

◀◀ **TYPE**: clastic sedimentary
COLOR: varied
TEXTURE: very mixed, with some big stones
MAIN MINERALS: quartz, flint, and chert pebbles
HOW FORMED: by fast-flowing rivers

Metamorphic rocks

Some rocks are transformed into completely new rocks by the crushing pressure of Earth's movements or by the heat of magma. These are metamorphic rocks.

Marble

Marble is a beautiful stone made by the metamorphism of limestone. It is pure white, or white with ripples. Marble is usually formed when magma cooks limestone (contact metamorphism). It can also be made by extreme pressure deep under mountains (regional metamorphism).

TYPE: contact or regional metamorphic
COLOR: white, often color-rippled
TEXTURE: sugary
MAIN MINERALS: calcite
HOW FORMED: limestone cooked by magma

Spotlight on marble

When cut and polished, marble turns shining white. It is perfect material for carved statues and for making buildings look good.

The Carrara quarries in Italy produce perfect white marble. The rock is extracted by drilling and sawing out huge blocks.

India's Taj Mahal was built from white marble by Mughal emperor Shah Jahan for the tomb of his wife, Mumtaz Mahal, in the 17th century.

Popular with sculptors, marble seems to have an inner glow. In 1922 Georgia marble was used for the statue in the Lincoln Memorial, Washington, DC.

The water is turned blue by silt washed out of glaciers

Marble halls

On the shore of Lake General Carrera, in southern Chile, marble has been worn into a series of beautiful caverns known as the Marble Cathedral.

The colors, swirls, and veins seen in many marbles are caused by impurities in the original limestone that was metamorphosed to form marble.

Skarn

Skarns are made when hot fluids bubbling up around magma completely dissolve limestone and dolostone. This is known as metasomatism. The results are rocks containing many minerals, including gems such as tourmaline, topaz, and beryl.

TYPE: metasomatic
COLOR: brown, black, varied
TEXTURE: varied
MAIN MINERALS: pyroxene, garnet, idocrase, wollastonite, actinolite
HOW FORMED: limestone dissolved by hot fluids

LOOK

shiny banded rock

small grains

Phyllite

High pressure turns shale first into slate and then into phyllite. The pressure causes mineral crystals to line up, producing glittery bands in the phyllite. This rock also has a silky sheen, known as phyllite luster.

TYPE: medium-grade regional metamorphic
COLOR: brown, black, varied
TEXTURE: very fine grained, banded
MAIN MINERALS: mica, chlorite, graphite
HOW FORMED: extreme pressure on shale or slate

Amphibolite

Amphibolite is a hard, glittery, dark greenish rock. Extreme heat and pressure turns basalt first into greenschist and then into amphibolite. Amphibolite does not develop bands.

TYPE: high-grade regional metamorphic
COLOR: black, dark green
TEXTURE: fine grained, unbanded
MAIN MINERALS: hornblende, amphibole, plagioclase feldspar
HOW FORMED: extreme pressure on basalt

TYPE: medium-grade regional metamorphic
COLOR: greenish-gray, black stripe
TEXTURE: fine to medium grained, banded
MAIN MINERALS: mica, chlorite
HOW FORMED: medium heat and pressure on phyllite

Granulite

Extreme heat and pressure creates high-grade metamorphic rocks—the most altered rocks of all. These rocks are extremely tough. High-grade granulite gets its name from its grainy look.

TYPE: high-grade regional metamorphic
COLOR: black, dark brown
TEXTURE: medium to coarse grained, unbanded
MAIN MINERALS: pyroxene, plagioclase feldspar
HOW FORMED: extreme heat and moderate pressure on basalt

Slate

Slate is a very smooth, dark stone made from the moderate metamorphism of shale and mudstone. It's brittle and can be easily split into thin layers.

Red slate

Gray slate

TYPE: low-grade regional metamorphic
COLOR: gray-green to black
TEXTURE: very fine grained, flaky
MAIN MINERALS: mica and chlorite
HOW FORMED: moderate heat and pressure on shale or mudstone

Schist

After shale has turned to slate and then to phyllite, it metamorphoses into schist. Pressure forces mica crystals to grow in line, creating distinctive gray or black stripes called schistosity.

Schists sometimes contain garnets

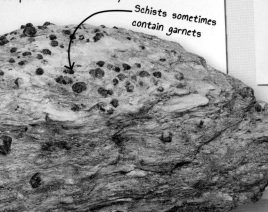

Quartzite

Quartzite looks a bit like brown marble. But it is made by the metamorphism of sandstone, not limestone, and it is mostly quartz. It's also tougher—you can't scratch it with a coin.

TYPE: contact or regional metamorphic
COLOR: pale brown or white
TEXTURE: sugary, medium grained
MAIN MINERALS: almost pure quartz
HOW FORMED: medium heat and pressure on sandstone

Fulgurite

Fulgurites are rare knobbly, glassy tubes that form when lightning strikes sand and fuses the sand into glass. Rock fulgurites occur where lightning blasts across the surface of rock and scorches a glassy mark, as on Oregon's Mount Thielsen.

TYPE: metamorphic
COLOR: gray-green, black
TEXTURE: glassy
MAIN MINERALS: silica mineral lechtalierite
HOW FORMED: lightning strike

Gneiss

Rugged gneiss (pronounced "nice") gets its name from the old German for "glittering." It forms under extreme heat and pressure, deep below mountains. It comes to the surface only when those mountains are worn away.

TYPE: high-grade regional metamorphic
COLOR: gray-green, black
TEXTURE: medium to coarse grained
MAIN MINERALS: mica and chlorite
HOW FORMED: extreme heat and pressure on any rock

Nice Nugget! The Christ the Redeemer statue that stands

Migmatite

Migmatites are the most extremely metamorphosed of all rocks. "Migma" means "mix," and these rocks are a mix of dark gneiss, schist, and amphibolite streaked with pale bands of igneous rock such as granite.

TYPE: extreme regional metamorphic
COLOR: varied
TEXTURE: medium, banded
MAIN MINERALS: typically gneiss with granite
HOW FORMED: extreme heat and pressure on metamorphosed rock

Hornfels

So-named because its shards look like animal horn, this hard rock forms when magma heats shales and other rocks. It can resemble basalt, but any spots confirm it is hornfels.

TYPE: medium-grade contact metamorphic
COLOR: black, bluish, grayish
TEXTURE: fine grained, non-banded
MAIN MINERALS: unidentifiable
HOW FORMED: contact of magma with many rocks

Serpentinite

Serpentinite is created by hot fluids getting into rocks such as peridotite and dunite and transforming them. The result is a snakeskin-like network of rare minerals, with studs of green.

> **TYPE**: hot-fluid metamorphic
> **COLOR**: gray-green to black
> **TEXTURE**: fine grained, banded
> **MAIN MINERALS**: serpentine minerals, olivine
> **HOW FORMED**: by hot fluids infiltrating rocks

Soapstone

Made mostly of talc, soft, white soapstone gets its name because it can feel almost like soap. It is made when pressure and hot fluids transform rocks that are very low in silica, such as dunite or serpentinite.

> **TYPE**: metasomatic and metamorphic
> **COLOR**: white
> **TEXTURE**: powdery
> **MAIN MINERALS**: talc
> **HOW FORMED**: by hot fluids acting on low-silica rocks

...bove Rio de Janeiro, Brazil, is partly made of **soapstone**.

Mylonite

Streaky mylonites form deep inside Earth, where rock is so hot it is too soft to shatter, so it's simply smeared out by the extreme pressure.

> **TYPE**: high-grade regional metamorphic
> **COLOR**: varied
> **TEXTURE**: fine grained, banded
> **MAIN MINERALS**: varies, but typically quartz and feldspar
> **HOW FORMED**: extreme pressure on hot, soft rock

LOOK

toffee-like streaks

fine grains

Rocks from space

Earth is under constant bombardment from space rocks. Most burn up in the atmosphere. Those that reach the ground are called meteorites.

The 160 ft- (50 m-) wide meteorite that formed this crater 50,000 years ago vaporized on impact.

Barringer Crater, Arizona

Very occasionally, a large meteorite strikes, blasting out a huge crater. Barringer Crater is 0.75 miles (1.2 km) wide.

IT'S AMAZING!

The Hoba meteorite in Namibia is the largest ever found. It is so heavy (at 60 tons) that it is still exactly where it landed!

Alien invaders!

Most meteorites are small chunks hurled out when asteroids collide. A few come from the moon and some from Mars.

Iron meteorites are made mainly of the metals iron and nickel. They are thought to be pieces from the iron cores of shattered asteroids.

Stony meteorites have a similar makeup to the rocks of Earth's mantle. Most space rocks that fall to Earth are stony meteorites.

This meteorite's surface is peppered with olivine crystals.

Stony-iron meteorites are made up of a mixture of iron, nickel, and silicate minerals. They often contain large crystals of olivine or pyroxene.

Tektites are glass lumps formed when a meteorite strikes Earth rocks. Rock is melted by the impact, flung into the air, and quickly cools into glass.

More rocks

Each rock has its own story to tell, written in its texture, color, pattern, mineral makeup, and where it's found.

Tillite (clastic sedimentary)

Siltstone (clastic sedimentary)

Red chalk (biochemical sedimentary)

Olivine gabbro (intrusive igneous)

Amphibolite with garnets (metamorphic)

Troctolite (intrusive igneous)

Snowflake obsidian (volcanic igneous)

Ferruginous sandstone (clastic sedimentary)

Luxullianite (intrusive igneous)

Green layered marble (metamorphic)

Staurolite schist (metamorphic)

Granite pegmatite (intrusive igneous)

Augen gneiss (metamorphic)

Oil shale (sedimentary)

Lava bomb (volcanic igneous)

69

Rock ID chart

Follow this chart to find out if a rock is igneous, sedimentary, or metamorphic. It will also give you clues to help you identify some major rock types.

GO TO PART 2
(Turn to page 72)

GO TO PART 3
(Turn to page 73)

PART 1

Does the rock contain a lot of crystals? You may need to look at it with a magnifying glass. — **NO**

YES

Can you see layers or bands of different shades or colors within the rock? — **NO** / **YES**

Is the entire rock a pale color? Try comparing it to other rocks. — **NO**

Can you see layers or bands of different shades or colors within the rock? — **YES**

Does the rock look crinkly, and is it full of shiny, flaky minerals? — **NO**

YES

When viewed without a magnifying glass, are the grains medium size, and is the rock pale gray? — **YES** / **NO**

Marble (pages 60–61)

Will the rock scratch glass? Lay the glass tile on a table and drag the rock over it. — **NO** / **YES**

Is the rock coarse grained (with crystals larger than rice grains) and a dark color? — **YES** / **NO**

Diorite (page 44)

Do you need a magnifying glass to see the grains of crystal in the rock? — **NO** / **YES**

Basalt (pages 32–33)

70

You will need:

Magnifying glass
Steel nail
Glass tile

Gneiss
(page 64)

Schist (page 63)

Granite (pages 40–41)

Is the rock coarse grained, with crystals that are mostly larger than grains of rice?

YES

NO

Rhyolite (page 34)

Gabbro (page 44)

Dolerite (page 45)

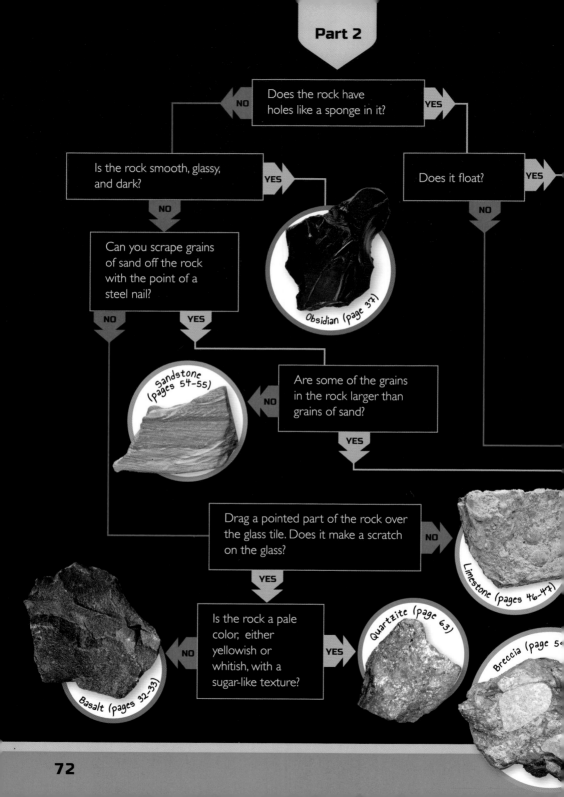

Part 2

Does the rock have holes like a sponge in it?

NO   **YES**

Is the rock smooth, glassy, and dark?   **YES**

Does it float?   **YES**

NO

NO

Can you scrape grains of sand off the rock with the point of a steel nail?

NO   **YES**

Obsidian (page 37)

Are some of the grains in the rock larger than grains of sand?

NO

YES

Sandstone (pages 54–55)

Drag a pointed part of the rock over the glass tile. Does it make a scratch on the glass?

NO

YES

Limestone (pages 46–47)

Is the rock a pale color, either yellowish or whitish, with a sugar-like texture?

NO   **YES**

Basalt (pages 32–33)

Quartzite (page 63)

Breccia (page 5...)

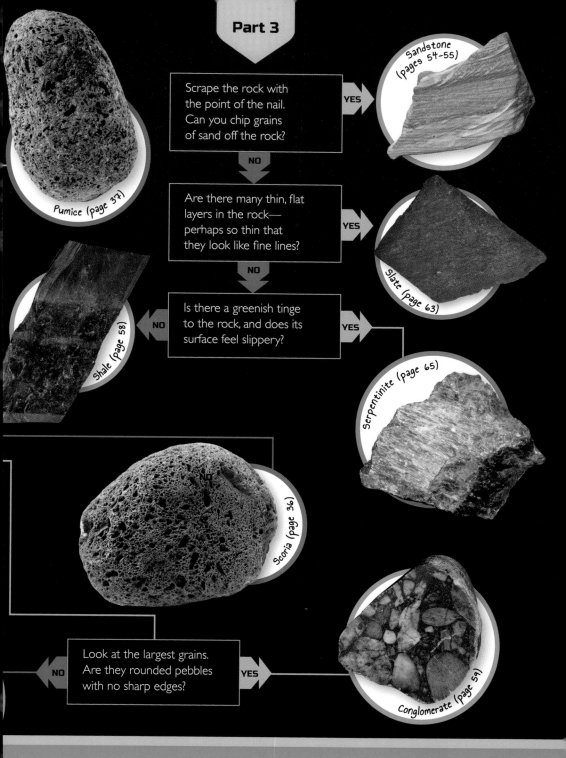

Part 3

Pumice (page 37)

Scrape the rock with the point of the nail. Can you chip grains of sand off the rock?

YES → Sandstone (pages 54–55)

NO ↓

Are there many thin, flat layers in the rock—perhaps so thin that they look like fine lines?

YES → Slate (page 63)

NO ↓

Is there a greenish tinge to the rock, and does its surface feel slippery?

NO ← Shale (page 58)

YES → Serpentinite (page 65)

Scoria (page 36)

Look at the largest grains. Are they rounded pebbles with no sharp edges?

NO ←

YES → Conglomerate (page 59)

Mineral hunting

Colossal crystals

The atoms in minerals are joined in regular patterns to make crystals. The Crystal Cave at Naica, Mexico, contains giant crystals up to 50 ft (15 m) long that grew slowly over 500,000 years. The crystals are made of selenite, a form of the mineral gypsum.

People love the dazzling beauty of mineral gems. But minerals also give us useful metals, fuel for our power stations, fertilizers for our crops, salt to flavor our food, and so much more.

Marvelous minerals

Minerals are the natural crystals from which all the world's rocks are made. There are more than 5,000 different kinds of mineral, but only 30 or so are really common. If you're lucky, you may find one of the rarer minerals.

Purple fluorite on quartz

Mineral crystals

Each mineral's crystals have a particular geometric shape. This shape fits into one of the six groups, or "crystal systems," shown below. Crystals rarely form in perfect shapes like these, but the crystals of a particular mineral typically grow together in their own distinctive way. This is known as the mineral's "habit" (see page 82).

CRYSTAL SYSTEMS

Trigonal/ hexagonal   Orthorhombic   Tetragonal   Triclinic

Monoclinic   Cubic

Chemical makeup

What makes each mineral unique is its chemistry—the chemical elements from which it's made. A few minerals, including gold, are made from just one element. Most are compounds, or combinations of two or more elements. Quartz, for example, is a compound of oxygen and silicon.

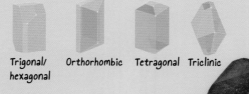

Gemstones are rare, large, sparkly mineral crystals that are hard enough to cut and shape into jewelry.

How minerals form

Mineral crystals don't form all at once but grow bit by bit in places where conditions are right. They either form anew from fluids or by the alteration of existing minerals.

  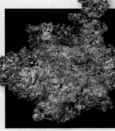 

As magmas cool, the chemicals in them join and grow together as crystals. Some of the best crystals form last in narrow veins, like this tourmaline in granite.

Minerals can form from dissolved chemicals when water evaporates from lagoons, lakes, and hot water springs such as Champagne Pool, New Zealand, shown above.

Chemicals in rocks can alter minerals and form new ones. So too can air, changing copper to malachite, for example, and so can water.

When metamorphic processes change rocks, new minerals can form. Pinkish red rubies, for example, are often found in the metamorphic rocks schist and gneiss.

Quartz stained red by hematite

Periodic Table

Just 118 elements make up everything in the universe, including all the rocks and minerals you will ever find.

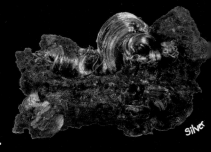

Silver

Scientists have categorized them into the Periodic Table.

1
H
HYDROGEN

Rocky elements

99.4 percent of all rocks and minerals are made from only nine elements. Check out these nine, highlighted by white boxes.

47
Ag
SILVER

47 - The atomic number shows how many protons are in each atom. A silver atom has 47 protons.

Ag - This is the symbol for silver.

3	4
Li	**Be**
LITHIUM	BERYLLIUM

11	12
Na	**Mg**
SODIUM	MAGNESIUM

19	20	21	22	23	24	25	26	27
K	**Ca**	**Sc**	**Ti**	**V**	**Cr**	**Mn**	**Fe**	**Co**
POTASSIUM	CALCIUM	SCANDIUM	TITANIUM	VANADIUM	CHROMIUM	MANGANESE	IRON	COBALT
37	38	39	40	41	42	43	44	45
Rb	**Sr**	**Y**	**Zr**	**Nb**	**Mo**	**Tc**	**Ru**	**Rh**
RUBIDIUM	STRONTIUM	YTTRIUM	ZIRCONIUM	NIOBIUM	MOLYBDENUM	TECHNETIUM	RUTHENIUM	RHODIUM
55	56	57–71	72	73	74	75	76	77
Cs	**Ba**	**La–Lu**	**Hf**	**Ta**	**W**	**Re**	**Os**	**Ir**
CESIUM	BARIUM	LANTHANOIDS	HAFNIUM	TANTALUM	TUNGSTEN	RHENIUM	OSMIUM	IRIDIUM
87	88	89–103	104	105	106	107	108	109
Fr	**Ra**	**Ac–Lr**	**Rf**	**Db**	**Sg**	**Bh**	**Hs**	**Mt**
FRANCIUM	RADIUM	ACTINOIDS	RUTHERFORDIUM	DUBNIUM	SEABORGIUM	BOHRIUM	HASSIUM	MEITNER

Of the nine major rock-forming elements, the "big two" are silicon and oxygen, which together account for 73 percent of Earth's crust.

57	58	59	60	61	62
La	**Ce**	**Pr**	**Nd**	**Pm**	**Sm**
LANTHANUM	CERIUM	PRASEODYMIUM	NEODYMIUM	PROMETHIUM	SAMARI
89	90	91	92	93	94
Ac	**Th**	**Pa**	**U**	**Np**	**Pu**
ACTINIUM	THORIUM	PROTACTINIUM	URANIUM	NEPTUNIUM	PLUTON

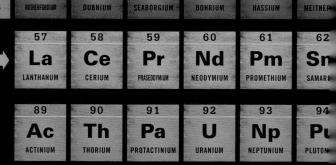

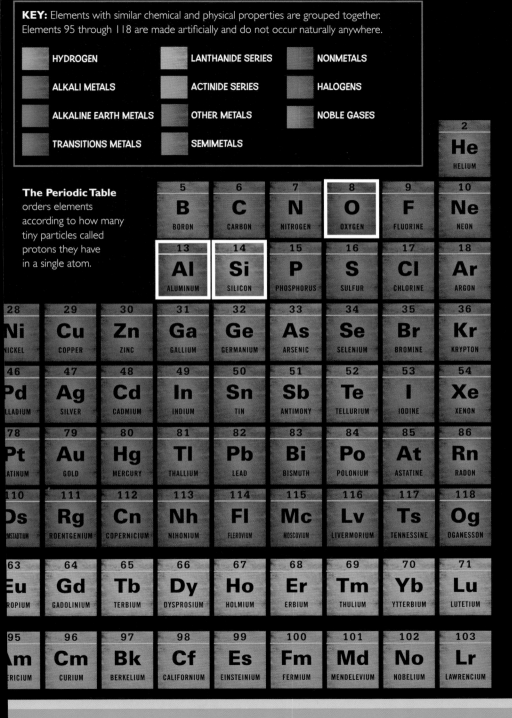

KEY: Elements with similar chemical and physical properties are grouped together. Elements 95 through 118 are made artificially and do not occur naturally anywhere.

HYDROGEN

ALKALI METALS

ALKALINE EARTH METALS

TRANSITIONS METALS

LANTHANIDE SERIES

ACTINIDE SERIES

OTHER METALS

SEMIMETALS

NONMETALS

HALOGENS

NOBLE GASES

The Periodic Table orders elements according to how many tiny particles called protons they have in a single atom.

79

Identifying minerals

Discovering what type of mineral you've found is like solving a puzzle. You'll have to gather the evidence yourself, but as you put the pieces of the puzzle together, your mystery mineral's identity will become clear!

Garnet in pegmatite

Where did you find it?

The first clue is the mineral's location. By learning about how and where different minerals form, you'll be able to tell which minerals you're likely to find in particular places. Rhodochrosite, for example, usually occurs in rock veins, while garnet and tourmaline are often found in pegmatites. Sulfur is typically found around volcanic vents and galena in limestone cliffs.

Check the rock!

The clue to a mineral's identity is often in the rock. If you find blue crystals, for example, look at the surrounding rock. If it's metamorphic, you've found kyanite; if it's sedimentary, you've got celestite.

Celestite

Kyanite

Step-by-step ID guide

Pages 80–85 will teach you the skills to make you a mineral super-sleuth! It's always best to carry out your investigations in the order shown here.

1. Where did you find it, and what minerals (if any) did you find it with?
2. Now look at its color and habit (see page 82). This should help you identify a few minerals.
3. Does its surface look metallic or nonmetallic (see page 83)?
4. Next, carry out a streak test (see page 83).
5. Then test the mineral's hardness (see page 84).
6. Finally, measure its specific gravity, or SG (see page 85).

Prime locations Here are some key minerals and the places they're typically found in.

IGNEOUS VEINS	PEGMATITES	RIVER SANDS	LIMESTONE CLIFFS	VOLCANIC DEBRIS	VOLCANIC VENTS
Sulfides such as pyrite	Quartz	Quartz	Calcite	Olivine	Sulfur
Copper minerals such as azurite and malachite	Feldspars	Gold	Fluorite	Augite	Sulfates such as gypsum, jarosite, thenardite
Gold and silver	Micas	Diamond	Galena	Amphibole	
	Sulfides such as siderite, apatite, beryl, amazonite, aquamarine, kunzite, zircon, chrysoberyl, emerald, garnet, lepidolite, topaz, spodumene, tourmaline	Emerald	Sphalerite		
		Cassiterite	Marcasite	Anorthite	Hematite

What did you find it with?

When you found your mineral, were there any other minerals nearby? If two or more minerals are usually found together, such as azurite and malachite, it's known as an "association." Getting to know common or easy-to-spot associations will help you find minerals. So if you see a blue mineral you recognize as azurite, there's a good chance you'll find green malachite nearby.

EASY-TO-SPOT ASSOCIATIONS:

blue azurite	◄——►	green malachite
purple fluorite	◄——►	black sphalerite
red garnet	◄——►	black mica
green amazonite	◄——►	smoky quartz
brassy pyrite	◄——►	milky quartz
green apatite	◄——►	orange calcite
golden-brown barite	◄——►	yellow calcite
purple amethyst	◄——►	colorless or golden calcite

What color is it?

Some minerals have distinctive colors that rarely change. Crysocolla, for example, is always blue and sulfur is always yellow. But be warned—color can throw you off the scent! When pure, many minerals are white or colorless. It's usually impurities (traces of other chemicals) in a mineral that give it its color, so two samples of the same mineral can look different.

CROCOITE (ALMOST ALWAYS SCARLET)

Long, thin crystals

FLUORITE (WIDE COLOR RANGE)

shape is it?

inerals have a perfect crystal shape, their system (see page 76), but they very rarely this perfect shape and often don't grow at all. "Habit" is the word used to describe mineral grows: as prism-shaped crystals, of needle-like crystals, in crusts, as powdery and in many other ways. Some habits are in the table to the right.

ACICULAR	needle-like clusters
BLADED	flat, slender, blade-like crystals
BOTRYOIDAL	rounded like grapes
DENDRITIC	branching like a tree
DRUSY	a thin, crusty coating
FIBROUS	very thin crystals like fibers
FOLIATED	layered, like overlapping leaves
GLOBULAR	shaped like balls
MASSIVE	masses, with no clear shape
RENIFORM	kidney-shaped
RUTILATED	needles inside another crystal
TABULAR	broad, flat crystals, like tabletops

Scolecite has an acicular habit, meaning that it grows in sprays of needles.

What's the surface like?

The appearance of a mineral's surface is called its luster. It depends on how the surface reflects light. Luster may be vitreous (glassy), metallic, submetallic (less reflective than metal), pearly, greasy, resinous (like resin or glue), silky, waxy, dull, earthy, or adamantine (sparkling like diamond).

Olivine has a vitreous, or glassy, luster.

Purple fluorite crystals are often confused with amethyst.

Does it make a streak?

Streak is the color of the mark left by a mineral when you scrape it across an unglazed ceramic tile (or the underside of a glazed tile). The streak will be the same color for every sample of the mineral, even if it is tarnished or discolored by impurities, so this is a useful test.

All graphite samples leave the same color streak.

Graphite leaves a black streak on an unglazed tile.

How hard is it?

A good clue to a mineral's identity is its hardness. Like streak, hardness is the same for all samples of the same mineral. The Mohs scale rates hardness from 1 (softest) to 10 (hardest), measured against the hardness of 10 standard example minerals. Minerals with a higher rating will scratch those with a lower rating.

Halite rates 2 on the Mohs scale. This means it is able to scratch talc (1) and can itself be scratched by calcite (3).

HARDNESS	MINERAL	SCRATCH TEST WITH HOUSEHOLD OBJECTS
1.	Talc (softest)	Easily scratched by a fingernail (2.5)
2.	Gypsum	Can be scratched by a fingernail
3.	Calcite	Can be scratched by a copper coin (3.5)
4.	Fluorite	Can be scratched by an iron nail (4.5)
5.	Apatite	Can be scratched by a knife (5.5)
6.	Orthoclase	Can be scratched by a steel file (6.5)
7.	Quartz	Can be scratched by an emery board (8.5)
8.	Topaz	Can be scratched by an emery board
9.	Corundum	Cuts glass and cannot be scratched by an emery board
10.	Diamond (hardest)	Cuts glass and cannot be scratched by any household object

If a penny scratches a mineral, the mineral's hardness is less than 3.5.

You can use these everyday materials to carry out hardness tests on your own minerals.

SAFE MINERAL TESTING! Some minerals contain harmful chemicals. Only test a mineral if an adult agrees, and always wash your hands afterwards. Look out for this sign on the dangerous minerals.

...heavier than water.

This is a measure of the mineral's specific gravity (SG) — how dense it is compared to water. SG is the most difficult thing to test, but sometimes it's the only way to identify a mineral. That's because a single mineral may come in many colors, it may not have a clear habit, and other minerals may have the same color of streak.

Finding specific gravity

You'll need a digital spring balance that can measure samples in grams. You can buy them fairly inexpensively.

1. Hang the mineral specimen on a spring balance. Record its weight as accurately as you can.
2. With the mineral still suspended from the balance, dunk the mineral into a big bowl of water. Record its weight now.
3. Find the difference between the two readings. Then divide the first reading by the difference. The result is the mineral's SG.

Does it glow?

Here's a fun test. When you view certain minerals, including fluorite, calcite, opal, gypsum, aragonite, and sodalite, under ultraviolet (UV) light in a dark room, they glow in extraordinary colors. This glow is called fluorescence. You can buy UV flashlights for just a few dollars, so it's easy to do this test in your own home.

Native elements

Most minerals are compounds—made of two or more elements. But some are just made up of a single element. These are often valuable, so hold on tight if you find one!

Platinum

One of the rarest of the precious metals, platinum is easily mistaken for silver. It's typically found as flakes or grains and occasionally nuggets, mostly mixed in with other metals such as iron and iridium.

Crack·ing up! Q. Where can you always find gold?

Silver

It's no wonder people love to turn silver into jewelry. When polished, it shines. Silver is usually found in wiry, curling, branching masses in veins in dark igneous rock, along with galena (lead ore), zinc, and copper.

▶▶ **TYPE**: native element
HABIT: wiry branching masses
COLOR: silver with black tarnish
LUSTER: metallic
STREAK: silver
HARDNESS: 2.5-3 **SG**: 10-12

Dig It!

Most silver is mined deep underground. When it is exposed to the air, it tarnishes almost black.

TYPE: native element
HABIT: grains or nuggets
COLOR: silver gray
LUSTER: metallic
STREAK: steel gray
HARDNESS: 4-4.5 **SG**: 14-19

Gold

Gold is almost always pure, never tarnishes, and always stays shiny. If you're lucky, you can find tiny grains and nuggets of pure gold naturally in veins in igneous rocks, along with quartz and sulfide minerals such as stibnite. You may also find grains and nuggets washed out of the rock into gravel in rivers.

TYPE: native element
HABIT: grains or nuggets
COLOR: golden
LUSTER: metallic
STREAK: golden yellow
HARDNESS: 2.5-3 **SG:** 19.3

A. In the dictionary!

IT'S AMAZING!
The world's biggest gold nugget, known as the *Welcome Stranger*, was found in Australia in 1869. It measured 24 by 12 in (61 by 31 cm). Today it would be worth about $4 million!

Diamond

Made of pure carbon, this dazzling gem is one of the hardest known substances and is at least a billion years old. Diamond formed hundreds of miles beneath the ground. It was dragged up to the surface in pipes of hot magma that cooled to form rocks called kimberlites and lamproites.

TYPE: native element
HABIT: cubic crystals
COLOR: colorless
LUSTER: adamantine (diamond-like)
STREAK: white
HARDNESS: 10 **SG**: 3.5

Copper

When exposed to the air, copper turns a vivid green, called copper bloom. But scrape the surface and you'll see the glowing copper beneath. Native copper was one of the first metals found and used, but it's now rare.

TYPE: native element
HABIT: cubic crystals
COLOR: copper, turns green when exposed to air
LUSTER: metallic
STREAK copper
HARDNESS: 2.5-3 **SG**: 8.9

Nice Nugget!

Sulfur is why onions make you cry, your pee is yellow, and rotten eggs smell stinky!

Iron

Native iron, known as telluric iron, is rare because it corrodes (rusts). The only deposit is in Greenland. Sometimes metallic iron can also be found in meteorites.

TYPE: native element
HABIT: masses
COLOR: gray
LUSTER: metallic
STREAK: gray
HARDNESS: 4 **SG**: 7.3-7.87

LOOK

bright yellow color

glassy crystals

Graphite is super-slippy. Flaky masses fall off and leave black marks—so it's perfect for pencils!

Graphite

Like diamond, graphite is pure carbon, but it is soft and made of black flakes. It is usually found in flaky masses in marble.

> **TYPE**: native element
HABIT: flaky masses
COLOR: black
LUSTER: metallic, dull
STREAK black
HARDNESS: 1-2 **SG**: 2.2

Arsenic

BEWARE of arsenic when looking for silver! This mineral is sometimes found alongside silver and it's very poisonous—fortunately, it is rare. Hit it with a hammer and it smells like garlic. Do not touch!

> **TYPE**: native element
HABIT: banded or kidney-shaped masses
COLOR: pale gray
LUSTER: metallic (dull when tarnished)
STREAK black
HARDNESS: 3-4 **SG**: 5.4-5.9

Bismuth

Most specimens of bismuth crystals you see are not found in the ground but grown in laboratories. Natural bismuth rarely forms crystals but is found as shapeless lumps with a rainbow sheen.

Sulfur

Crusts of sulfur form around fumaroles (little chimneys on volcanoes) and around hot volcanic springs—and they often smell like rotten eggs. But most commercial sulfur is found in beds in limestone and gypsum.

> **TYPE**: native element
HABIT: crusts and powders
COLOR: yellow
LUSTER: vitreous (glassy) or earthy
STREAK whitish yellow
HARDNESS: 2 **SG**: 2-2.1

> **TYPE**: native element
HABIT: chunks and nuggets
COLOR: silvery white, with a rainbow tarnish
LUSTER: metallic
STREAK greenish black
HARDNESS: 2-2.5 **SG**: 9.7-9.8

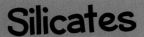

Silicates

It's a silicate world! A third of all common minerals are silicates, and silicates make up 90 percent of Earth's crust. Most are ultra-tough and last long after the rock they formed in has disintegrated.

Quartz

Super-common quartz is the key ingredient in most igneous and metamorphic rocks, and in sedimentary sandstones. It mostly occurs as tiny grains, but also forms stunning crystals.

Crystal magic

Spectacular quartz crystals—such as these amethyst crystals—can form under special conditions, for example in geodes.

IT'S AMAZING!

Battery watches all have a quartz crystal in them. Electrical charges make the crystal vibrate at exactly 32,768 times per second, and that keeps the time!

Spotlight on quartz

Pure quartz is as colorless as glass. But impurities can give it a huge variety of colors, from purple amethyst to yellow citrine.

Traces of iron and radiation turn quartz to purple amethyst.

Smoky quartz is one of the few brown gemstones. The color comes from the exposure of quartz to radiation underground.

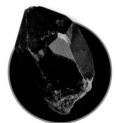

Rose quartz is a beautiful and very common pink form of quartz. It gets its pink coloring from traces of the oxide mineral rutile.

Milky quartz is turned white by tiny drops of fluid trapped inside the crystals. It may occur with gold, so gold prospectors look for milky quartz in the hope of striking it rich!

Rock crystal is clear, colorless quartz. It's the least expensive of gems, as it's so common. Huge crystals of it were once used to make fortune tellers' crystal balls.

Tourmaline

In ancient Egypt, this mineral was called "rainbow rock," as a single tourmaline crystal can be multicolored. Look out for crystals with many colors and a column shape.

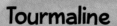
LÓÒK

crystals are often triangular in cross-section

▶▶ **TYPE**: silicate
HABIT: typically six-sided prisms
COLOR: variable, from blue-black to green and pink
LUSTER: vitreous (glassy)
STREAK: white
HARDNESS: 7.5 **SG**: 3-3.2

Beryl

Formed in quartz feldspar or in cavities from mineral-rich water, beryl gives us a range of gems. Blue beryl is aquamarine, yellow beryl is heliodore, and pink beryl is morganite. Add a little chrome and vanadium, and you get green emerald!

▶▶ **TYPE**: silicate
HABIT: six-sided crystals, sometimes gigantic
COLOR: variable, from gold to pink
LUSTER: vitreous (glassy)
STREAK: white
HARDNESS: 7.5-8 **SG**: 2.6-2.9

Topaz

Topaz is a dense, super-tough gem. Often found with fluorite in pegmatites, it may be colorless or have pale hues, such as pinks and yellows.

◀◀ **TYPE**: silicate
HABIT: usually prism-shaped crystals
COLOR: colorless, or pale yellows and pinks
LUSTER: vitreous (glassy)
STREAK: white.
HARDNESS: 8 **SG**: 3.5-3.6

Garnet

Garnet is a tough gem formed by huge pressures under mountains in rocks such schist. There are over 20 varieties, including ruby-red spessartine and purplish-red almandine.

🔺 **TYPE**: silicate
HABIT: diamond- or trapezoid-shaped crystals
COLOR: dark red or green
LUSTER: vitreous (glassy)
STREAK: white
HARDNESS: 6.5-7.5 **SG**: 3.5

Nice Nugget!

Garnet gets its name because red garnets look like red pomegranate seeds.

Olivine

Olivine is a key ingredient in the rock peridotite, which forms much of Earth's interior. But it's also occasionally found as tiny grains in basalt and gabbro. And rarest of all is when it occurs as olive-green gem crystals called peridots.

▶▶ **TYPE**: silicate
HABIT: short prisms
COLOR: olive-green
LUSTER: vitreous (glassy)
STREAK: white
HARDNESS: 6.5-7 **SG**: 3.5

Opal

Rainbow-hued opal is Australia's national gem, because so much of it is found there. It is not a crystal like other minerals, but a hardened gel of silica that can form in cracks just about anywhere.

LOOK

opal shimmers in the light

▶▶ **TYPE**: silicate
HABIT: diamond- or trapezoid-shaped crystals
COLOR: red
LUSTER: vitreous (glassy)
STREAK: white
HARDNESS: 6.5-7.5 **SG**: 3.5

🔺 **TYPE**: silicate
HABIT: hardened gel
COLOR: rainbow
LUSTER: vitreous (glassy), waxy
STREAK: white
HARDNESS: 6.5-7.5 **SG**: 3.5

Pyrope

Ruby-red pyrope is a kind of garnet that gets its name from the Greek for "fire" and "eye." It's very rare, but it is sometimes found in river gravel or embedded in rocks such as dunite and peridotite.

Chalcedony

Chalcedony is a beautiful, gem-like form of the rock chert. It does not form large crystals but is "cryptocrystalline," which means that it forms in masses of crystals so tiny they can only be seen under a microscope.

TYPE: silicate
HABIT: cryptocrystalline (crystals too small to be seen)
COLOR: many colors
LUSTER: vitreous (glassy) or resinous
STREAK: white
HARDNESS: 7 **SG**: 2.65

Rock   Star!

Chalcedony may have been one of the first materials humans ever used—they shaped it into arrowheads.

Jasper

Jasper is the opaque variety of chalcedony. It forms as agate nodules, but you can also find it as pebbles on the beach, which glow red or green when wet.

TYPE: silicate
HABIT: cryptocrystalline (crystals too small to be seen)
COLOR: usually red or green
LUSTER: resinous
STREAK: white
HARDNESS: 7 **SG**: 2.65

Onyx

Onyx is a striped variety of agate. It forms naturally near the bottom of agate nodules. Cameos (miniature pictures in jewelry) are often made of onyx.

TYPE: silicate
HABIT: cryptocrystalline (crystals too small to be seen)
COLOR: dark and light stripes
LUSTER: resinous
STREAK: white
HARDNESS: 7
SG: 2.65

Nice Nugget!

Scenic agate looks like a ferny woodland scene!

Agate

Agate is another type of chalcedony. It forms nodules in cavities in basalt when traces of iron, manganese, and other chemicals create ring-like bands in the chalcedony. There are many varieties, including blue lace agate.

TYPE: silicate
HABIT: cryptocrystalline
COLOR: concentric colored bands, often brown
LUSTER: resinous
STREAK: white
HARDNESS: 7 **SG**: 2.65

Orthoclase

The two kinds of feldspar are orthoclase and plagioclase. Orthoclase is based on potassium, and plagioclase on sodium and calcium. Together, these two minerals make up two-thirds of Earth's crust. Moonstones are rare orthoclase gems with a shimmering colored surface.

TYPE: silicate
HABIT: typically massive, but may form tablet-chaped crystals
COLOR: off-white
LUSTER: vitreous (glassy)
STREAK: white
HARDNESS: 6
SG: 2.53

Rock Star!

Most of the ceramicware in your home is made from orthoclase feldspar.

Albite

Albite is a type of plagioclase with slightly more sodium. Its name comes from the Latin "albus," ("white"). Anorthite is a type of plagioclase with slightly more calcium.

TYPE: silicate
HABIT: mostly massive, but may form twinned crystals
COLOR: white
LUSTER: vitreous (glassy)
STREAK: white
HARDNESS: 6-6.5
SG: 2.63 (albite), 2.76 (anorthite)

Sodalite

Sodalite is a "feldspathoid," which means it's similar to feldspar but contains two-thirds less silica. This blue mineral is fluorescent, glowing vividly under ultraviolet (UV) light.

LOOK

intense blue color ——

greasy luster ——

TYPE: silicate
HABIT: usually massive, but may form crystals
COLOR: blue, white, gray
LUSTER: vitreous (glassy) or greasy
STREAK: white
HARDNESS: 5.5-6   **SG**: 2.1-2.3

Geodes

Don't ignore dull, round stones—they could be geodes. Crack one open and you might reveal an amazing treasure chest of sparkling crystals!

Hidden gem

If you find a bumpy round stone like a large potato, tap it with a hammer. If it sounds hollow, it could be a geode! This one is lined with agate and quartz.

Sliced and polished geode

IT'S AMAZING!

In 2000, geologists found a huge geode in an old silver mine near Almeria in Spain. It was so big you could climb inside it!

Hidden worlds

A geode forms when a gas pocket in rock slowly fills with mineral-rich fluid and then gradually dries out. As it dries out, crystals grow in layers around the inner walls.

Agate bands

Amethyst crystals

Most geodes fill with crystals of quartz or calcite. Traces of different chemicals create different colors. Iron, for example, gives beautiful amethyst—a purple form of quartz.

Mineral suppliers use special tools to cut flat across a geode, then polish the surface to reveal the beautiful bands within.

A thunder egg is baseball sized. Inside it looks like a filled-in geode, with no hollows. It begins as a gas bubble in rhyolite lava, then fills with layers of minerals, usually chalcedony.

Weathering frees geodes from the surrounding rock.

Lazurite

A stunning, rich sky-blue color, there's no mineral like lazurite. It is the major ingredient in the blue gem lapis lazuli, which has been mined since ancient times in Afghanistan's Kokcha Valley.

TYPE: silicate
HABIT: masses or six-sided column crystals
COLOR: blue
LUSTER: greasy to dull
STREAK: white
HARDNESS: 5-5.6 **SG**: 2.6

LOOK

white and cloud-like

often no crystals

Nepheline

Nepheline gets its name from the Greek for "cloud," because white masses of it can look a little like fluffy clouds. It's a feldspathoid—like feldspar but with less silica.

TYPE: silicate
HABIT: masses and grains, and rare column-shaped crystals
COLOR: off-white
LUSTER: greasy or dull
STREAK: white
HARDNESS: 5.5-6 **SG**: 2.6

Heulandite

Heulandite is a "zeolite," a clay-like mineral with a special honeycomb crystal structure. It forms when bubbles left by hot fluids dry out and are altered heat and pressure.

TYPE: silicate
HABIT: coffin-shaped crystals
COLOR: mostly creamy white, also pink, brown
LUSTER: pearly or vitreous (glassy)
STREAK: white
HARDNESS: 3.5-4 **SG**: 2.1-2.3

Rock Star!

The honeycombed zeolites act like sponges and soak up polluting chemicals!

Stilbite

Stilbite is a zeolite that often grows in amazing crystals shaped like wheat sheaves or piles of bow ties. The crystals typically form where there have been large floods of basalt lava, such as in the Deccan Traps of India.

Diopside

Diopside is a pyroxene mineral, which means that it formed in lava while the lava was still hot. It's named for the Greek for "double vision," because when you look through some diopside crystals you see a double image.

In ancient China, that a piece of jade it was said to be more valuable than 15 cities.

Nice Nugget!

Jadeite

Jadeite, with nephrite, is one of the two beautiful green minerals called jade, long treasured in China and South America. Jadeite is a deeper green than nephrite and is more highly valued. Jadeite is most likely to be found as water-worn pebbles.

Augite

Augite forms dark greenish-brown, blocky, prism-shaped crystals. The crystals typically form in basalt lavas, and big crystals can often be found in the weathered lavas of Italian volcanoes.

> **TYPE**: silicate
> **HABIT**: typically stubby prisms
> **COLOR**: dark greenish-brown
> **LUSTER**: vitreous (glassy) to dull
> **STREAK**: greenish white
> **HARDNESS**: 5-6 **SG**: 3.2-3.6

Spodumene

Ash-gray spodumene gets its name from the Greek word "spodumenos" meaning "burned to ashes." It is the main ore of the super-light metal lithium, and it's found mostly in pegmatites.

> **TYPE**: silicate
> **HABIT**: usually masses, but sometimes long striped prisms
> **COLOR**: white or grayish white
> **LUSTER**: vitreous (glassy)
> **STREAK**: white
> **HARDNESS**: 6.5-7 **SG**: 3-3.2

Nice Nugget! Spodumene crystals can be over 50 ft (15 m) long and weigh 99 tons!

LOOK

blocky crystals

Andalusite

Andalusite is usually found in rounded, water-worn pebbles, although its crystals are square. Andalusite is very heat resistant, so it's often used in kilns, furnaces, and high-temperature industrial processes.

> **TYPE**: silicate
> **HABIT**: usually square crystals
> **COLOR**: russet-red, green and gold
> **LUSTER**: vitreous (glassy)
> **STREAK**: white
> **HARDNESS**: 7.5 **SG**: 3.1-3.2

Sphene

Sphene's name means "wedge" in Greek, and that's the shape of its crystals. It's also called titanite, because it's rich in the metal titanium. Sphene's soft but sparkling gem crystals can be found in narrow cracks in schist.

> **TYPE**: silicate
> **HABIT**: masses, sometimes wedge-shaped crystals
> **COLOR**: brown, green, or yellow
> **LUSTER**: adamantine (diamond-like)
> **STREAK**: white
> **HARDNESS**: 5-5.5 **SG**: 3.3-3.6

TYPE: silicate
HABIT: striped prism-shaped crystals
COLOR: pistachio green
LUSTER: vitreous (glassy)
STREAK: white to gray
HARDNESS: 6-7   **SG**: 3.3-3.5

Epidote

Epidote is known for its pistachio green crystals. It forms in metamorphic rocks, and if you're very lucky, you might find epidote alongside garnets in rocks such as schists and skarns.

⚠ Actinolite

Actinolite and closely related tremolite often come as long bladed crystals or felt-like masses called "mountain leather." BEWARE: they often form dangerous asbestos fibers. Keep them away from your face and immediately wash your hands if you touch them.

TYPE: silicate
HABIT: long, bladed or prism crystals, or fibrous masses
COLOR: white, grayish green
LUSTER: vitreous (glassy) or silky
STREAK: white
HARDNESS: 5-6   **SG**: 2.9-3.4

Dig It!

Actinolite fibers were used in the fireproof material asbestos, until they were found to be deadly!

Chlorite

Chlorite is one of the super-soft, super-absorbent "clay" minerals. Chlorite gets its name from the Greek for green, and that's its typical color. Chlorite forms soft, flaky masses from powdery materials made when the weather causes aluminum and magnesium silicates to crumble.

TYPE: silicate
HABIT: mostly scaly flakes
COLOR: usually green
LUSTER: vitreous (glassy), dull, peachy
STREAK: pale green, grayish
HARDNESS: 2-3
SG: 2.6-3.4

Serpentine

Serpentine gets its name because greenish flakes of it can look like snakeskin. It's found with talc where veins of hot fluid alter magnesium silicate in rocks such as peridotites and dolomites.

LÒÒK

feels greasy

TYPE: silicate
HABIT: fine-grained, flaky masses
COLOR: green, blue, yellow
LUSTER: waxy or greasy
STREAK: white
HARDNESS: 2.5   **SG**: 2.5-2.6

Talc

Talc is the softest of all minerals. It forms with serpentine in peridotite, dolomite, and other rocks when magnesium silicate is altered by hot fluids.

Rock Star!

Talcum powder, made from talc, absorbs moisture and odors. It's great for smelly feet!

TYPE: silicate
HABIT: fine-grained, flaky masses
COLOR: white, greenish
LUSTER: dull, pearly, greasy
STREAK: white
HARDNESS: 1   **SG**: 2.7-2.8

Biotite

Micas such as biotite and muscovite are important rock-forming minerals. Biotite mica is so soft you can scratch it with your fingernail. It does form crystals, but more often it's found as black flakes in rocks such as granite.

▶▶ **TYPE**: silicate
HABIT: mostly flakes, rarely six-sided crystals
COLOR: black, dark brown
LUSTER: vitreous (glassy) to pearly
STREAK: white
HARDNESS: 2.5 **SG**: 2.9-3.4

Muscovite

Muscovite is the most common type of mica, found in nearly all igneous and metamorphic rocks. It forms when feldspars are altered by heat and pressure. It's much lighter in color than biotite mica— often almost transparent.

▶▶ **TYPE**: silicate
HABIT: mostly flakes, rarely six-sided crystals
COLOR: purple to pink
LUSTER: vitreous (glassy) to pearly
STREAK: white
HARDNESS: 2.5 **SG**: 2.8

Lepidolite

Rare lepidolite can be so pretty and pink it's easy to forget that it's a kind of mica, like biotite. It forms only in granite pegmatite dikes, and only when there's a lot of lithium around.

Dig It!
Muscovite gets is name from Muscovy, the old name for Russia. It was used to make windows there long ago.

◀◀ **TYPE**: silicate
HABIT: mostly flakes, rarely six-sided crystals
COLOR: white, silver, brown
LUSTER: vitreous (glassy) to pearly
STREAK: white
HARDNESS: 2-2.5 **SG**: 2.8

More silicates

Silicates give us some of the most beautifully colored minerals in the world, often used in jewelry. Check out these little sparklers!

Emerald

Thomsonite

Pentagonite

Zircon

Cupro-austinite

Scolecite

Dioptase

Kyanite

Kammererite

Okenite

Apophyllite

Labradorite

Aquamarine

Gyrolite

Orthoclase feldspar

Amazonite

Vesuvianite

105

Carbonates, nitrates, & borates

Carbonates are a group of about 80 minerals. They are typically pale or clear, and soft or brittle. They form when a metal joins with carbon and oxygen. Nitrates and borates have a similar chemical structure.

Calcite

Calcite is one of the world's most common minerals. It is a key part of bones and animal shells, and it's the white crust that forms in teapots. Marble, chalk, and limestone are mostly calcite.

This specimen is partly stained red by hematite.

Bunch of nails

Nailhead spar is a type of calcite crystal in which the ends of the crystals look like the blunt tops of old nails.

Under normal light, calcite is white or clear.

Under UV light, calcite glows with bright color—typically red but also other colors, including green.

These crystals are known as "butterfly twins."

TYPE: carbonate
HABIT: mostly large masses, but also a wide variety of crystals
COLOR: white or clear
LUSTER: vitreous (glassy)
STREAK: white
HARDNESS: 3 **SG**: 2.7

Spotlight on calcite

Although most calcite is found in white masses, it also comes in an incredible range of clear or yellowish crystals. In fact, it can form over 300 different kinds of crystal—more than any other mineral. The crystals form in limestone caves, hydrothermal veins, and rock fissures (cracks).

Calcite crystals often come in a chunky, pointed shape as shown here—a shape described as "trigonal."

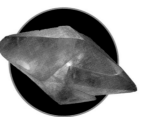

Dogtooth spar is often found in pools in limestone caves. It forms clusters of big crystals that look like dogs' teeth.

Iceland spar is a clear calcite crystal that resembles a block of ice. Look through it and you see a double image!

Looking closer...
The best place to see calcite is in limestone caves. Here, the slow dripping or ponding of calcite-rich water, dissolved from the limestone, creates spectacular formations.

Magnesite

Magnesite sometimes looks a little like porcelain and can be difficult to tell apart from calcite. It is magnesium carbonate and is the main ore for the metal magnesium. It typically forms when hot water alters magnesium minerals such as serpentine in limestone and dolostone.

▶ **TYPE**: carbonate
HABIT: fine-grained, porcelain-like masses
COLOR: white, gray
LUSTER: vitreous (glassy) to dull
STREAK: white
HARDNESS: 3.5-4 **SG**: 3

▲ **TYPE**: carbonate
HABIT: masses, druses (encrustations), and stalactites
COLOR: raspberry-pink
LUSTER: vitreous (glassy) to resinous
STREAK: white
HARDNESS: 3.5-4 **SG**: 3.5

Nice Nugget! Malachite was used by the ancient Egyptians

Siderite

Siderite is brown with a distinctive white streak. Like most carbonates, siderite is quite a soft mineral. It is iron carbonate, and forms where iron-rich fluids alter limestone.

▼ **TYPE**: carbonate
HABIT: earthy masses, rarely curved-bladed crystals
COLOR: dark brown
LUSTER: vitreous (glassy)
STREAK: white
HARDNESS: 3.5-4.5 **SG**: 3.9

Rhodochrosite

There is no mineral quite so distinctive as rhodochrosite. It can be brownish on the surface, but good crystals are a vivid raspberry pink. Rhodochrosite is manganese carbonate and it usually forms in hydrothermal veins.

TYPE: carbonate
HABIT: knobby clusters
COLOR: green, yellow, purple-pink
LUSTER: pearly to vitreous (glassy)
STREAK: white
HARDNESS: 4-4.5 **SG**: 4.4

as green paint on their tomb walls.

Smithsonite

Bumpy crusts of yellow smithsonite can look like raw turkey skin! It was once one of the main ores for zinc. It forms when exposure to the weather alters minerals such as sphalerite.

LOOK

bumpy crust

Dig It!

Malachite is often found inside stalactites and stalagmites. Slice one and you may find beautiful green growth rings.

Malachite

Malachite is a vivid green mineral formed when copper minerals are exposed to the air. The green tarnish you often see on bronze statues, known as verdigris, is malachite. Malachite can occur as needles, or as green masses where carbonated water comes into contact with copper.

TYPE: carbonate
HABIT: rounded masses, or tufts of needles
COLOR: bright green
LUSTER: vitreous (glassy) to dull in masses, silky crystals
STREAK: pale green
HARDNESS: 3.5-4 **SG**: 4

Azurite

Azurite is an unmistakably brilliant blue. Like malachite, it is made when copper minerals are weathered, but water in the crystals turns them blue.

> **TYPE**: carbonate
> **HABIT**: needles or velvety masses
> **COLOR**: deep blue
> **LUSTER**: vitreous (glassy) to dull
> **STREAK**: sky blue
> **HARDNESS**: 3.5-4 **SG**: 3.7

Aragonite

The aragonites are a group of minerals that look a lot like calcite. They include witherite and cerussite, as well as aragonite itself. It often forms stalactites and crusts around hot springs.

Dig It!

Look for pearl mussel and oyster shells on the beach. The mother-of-pearl lining is partly aragonite.

> **TYPE**: carbonate
> **HABIT**: prisms, wedges, and flower-like
> **COLOR**: white or clear
> **LUSTER**: vitreous (glassy) to dull
> **STREAK**: white
> **HARDNESS**: 3.5-4 **SG**: 2.9-3

Nice Nugget! In Renaissance times, artists ground up azurite

Cerussite

Cerussite is a dense mineral made from lead rather than calcium, typically found where lead ores are exposed to the air. It's famous for its brilliant crystals, which sparkle like lead-crystal glass and often come in distinctive pairs, or "twins."

> **TYPE**: carbonate
> **HABIT**: grainy masses or twinned crystals
> **COLOR**: white or clear
> **LUSTER**: adamantine (diamond-like) to dull
> **STREAK**: white
> **HARDNESS**: 3.5-3.75 **SG**: 6.5

Strontianite

Strontianite is a form of aragonite that is made from the rare metal strontium rather than calcium. It's typically found as spiky tufts of needles. Crystals of strontianite are uncommon. It is fluorescent in the dark under ultraviolet light, glowing yellow.

▶▶ **TYPE**: carbonate
HABIT: grainy masses or tufts of needles
COLOR: white or clear
LUSTER: vitreous (glassy) to greasy
STREAK: white
HARDNESS: 3.5-4 **SG**: 3.7

Witherite

Witherite is a form of aragonite made from barium rather than calcium. Its rare crystals are prized for their "twinning." This means that crystals branch into pairs.

▶▶ **TYPE**: carbonate
HABIT: triplets or twinned crystals
COLOR: white or clear
LUSTER: vitreous (glassy) to dull
STREAK: white
HARDNESS: 3.5-4 **SG**: 3.7

to make a **blue paint.**

Dolomite

Dolomite is the main mineral in a type of sedimentary rock that's also known as dolomite (or dolostone). Its crystals form in marbles and also in veins of hot fluid that are rich in magnesium. Dolomite can look very similar to calcite.

◀◀ **TYPE**: carbonate
HABIT: masses and saddle-shaped twinned crystals
COLOR: pink or gray
LUSTER: vitreous (glassy) to dull
STREAK: white
HARDNESS: 3.5-4 **SG**: 2.86

Ankerite

Ankerite is a form of dolomite in which the main metal is iron. It also contains magnesium and manganese. Ankerite is often found in ironstone.

▶▶ **TYPE**: carbonate
HABIT: curved diamond-shaped crystals, masses
COLOR: brown, dirty white
LUSTER: pearly
STREAK: white
HARDNESS: 3.5-4 **SG**: 3-3.1

Boracite

Boracite crystals are found in dry regions embedded in layers of anhydrite, gypsum, and halite. Although they look almost good enough to be gems, boracite crystals are rarely used for jewelry, because they dissolve too easily in water.

Borax

Borax is found naturally in dry regions, where it forms from the evaporation of salt lakes. Crystals are rare, and as soon as they dry out, they crumble to a white powder called tincalconite.

▲ **TYPE**: borate
HABIT: masses or, rarely, prismatic (prism-shaped) crystals
COLOR: colorless, blue to white
LUSTER: greasy
STREAK: white
HARDNESS: 2-2.5 **SG**: 1.7

▲ **TYPE**: borate
HABIT: chunky, often cubic crystals
COLOR: colorless, light blue, green
LUSTER: vitreous (glassy)
STREAK: white
HARDNESS: 7.5 **SG**: 2.9-3

Nitratine

Nitratine, also known as Chile saltpeter, was once used for fertilizers. It is only found in very dry regions because it quickly dissolves in the smallest amount of water, even damp air. Specimens must be stored in airtight containers.

▶ **TYPE**: nitrate
HABIT: mass of grainy crusts
COLOR: colorless, yellow to white
LUSTER: vitreous (glassy)
STREAK: white
HARDNESS: 1.5-2 **SG**: 2.2

Phosphates, arsenates, & vanadates

These three groups include minerals that contain dazzling crystals! They also include rare elements such as yttrium and cesium.

Turquoise

This vividly colored gemstone gets its blue-green color from traces of copper. Because it is solid and opaque, you might think it is just a mass. In fact, turquoise is cryptocrystalline, meaning that it's made up of tiny crystals too small for the eye to see.

TYPE: phosphate
HABIT: cryptocrystalline nodules and crusts
COLOR: turqoise
LUSTER: dull to waxy
STREAK: white with a hint of green
HARDNESS: 5-6 **SG:** 2.6-2.8

...corated with turquoise.

Wavellite

Wavellite forms fantastic starburst clusters of needle-shaped crystals. The clusters may grow into half-globes. It grows in veins of hot fluid in limestone, along with limonite, quartz, and micas.

TYPE: phosphate
HABIT: radiating needles
COLOR: yellow green, white
LUSTER: vitreous (glassy)
STREAK: white
HARDNESS: 3.5-4 **SG:** 2.3

LOOK

starbursts of radiating needles

Pyromorphite

Pyromorphite is a lead mineral which develops when other lead minerals near to phosphorus are exposed to air. Its name comes from the Greek "pyr" (meaning "fire") and "morph" ("form")—because when you heat it, its crystals reform!

▶▶ **TYPE**: phosphate
HABIT: slender hollow-ended crystals, or crusts
COLOR: greeny yellow
LUSTER: resinous to greasy
STREAK: off-white
HARDNESS: 3.5-4 **SG**: 7

Dig It!

Watch out! Vivianite starts out colorless, turns blue when exposed to air, then turns black if exposed for too long!

Vivianite

Vivianite forms in iron-ore veins and pegmatites. Vivianite crystals are often found inside fossil shells or attached to fossil bone.

▲ **TYPE**: phosphate
HABIT: radiating clusters, crusts, and in fossil shells
COLOR: blue, indigo, but darkening
LUSTER: vitreous (glassy)
STREAK: white or bluish green
HARDNESS: 1.5-2 **SG**: 2.6-2.7

Nice Nugget!

BEWARE! Torbernite is packed with uranium, which

▼ **TYPE**: phosphate
HABIT: small hexagonal prisms
COLOR: red, orange
LUSTER: adamantine (diamond-like), resinous
STREAK: brownish-yellow
HARDNESS: 3-4
SG: 6.7-7.1

Vanadinite

Vanadinite is an uncommon reddish-orange mineral that was once an important source of the rare metal vanadium. You can often find it together with lead minerals such as galena and wulfenite.

Erythrite

Erythrite typically occurs as a crust, called "cobalt bloom," on minerals containing cobalt. For miners, erythrite's striking red or pink color was once like a magic marker pointing to veins of the metal cobalt in the rock.

TYPE: phosphate
HABIT: crusts, occasionally needle-like crystals
COLOR: crimson to pink
LUSTER: vitreous (glassy)
STREAK: pale red
HARDNESS: 1.5-2.5 **SG**: 3

Autunite

Avoid autunite! Like torbernite, it's packed with uranium, and is radioactive. You can identify it by its greenish yellow square crystals and its combination with granite and torbernite.

TYPE: phosphate
HABIT: square tablets that stack like books
COLOR: greenish yellow
LUSTER: vitreous (glassy) to pearly
STREAK: pale green
HARDNESS: 2-2.5 **SG**: 3.2

Torbernite

Avoid torbernite! It contains uranium and is radioactive. It forms dark green square crystals and is found in combination with granite and autunite.

is used for **nuclear** power!

TYPE: phosphate
HABIT: square tablets that stack like books
COLOR: dark green
LUSTER: vitreous to pearly
STREAK: pale green
HARDNESS: 2-2.5 **SG**: 3.2

Variscite

This rare green mineral forms where phosphate-rich fluids react with aluminum-rich rocks. It is cryptocrystalline (made up of tiny crystals too small for the eye to see).

TYPE: phosphate
HABIT: cryptocrystalline nodules and crusts
COLOR: green
LUSTER: vitreous (glassy) to waxy
STREAK: white
HARDNESS: 4.5 **SG**: 2.6

Oxides
& hydroxides

Oxides are minerals made from oxygen and a metal. There are lots of them, which is lucky as they can produce beautiful gems! Hydroxides are oxides with hydrogen.

Rubies can vary from almost pink to nearly purple.

Ruby red

When corundum contains a tiny amount of chromium, it produces stunning purplish red rubies. Rubies often form in marble, but they're so tough they survive long after the marble crumbles.

IT'S AMAZING!
The blood-red rubies of Burma are known as pigeon-blood rubies. They're found in rivers where they were washed after being eroded out of marble.

Corundum

In extreme conditions, aluminum and oxygen combine to make corundum, one of the hardest minerals on Earth. It occurs as super-hard crystals, but often when exposed to the air it crumbles to a powder called black sand.

▼ **TYPE**: oxide
HABIT: powdery masses, or six-sided crystals
COLOR: brown or black
LUSTER: vitreous (glassy)
STREAK: white
HARDNESS: 9 **SG**: 4

Spotlight on corundum

Add a trace of a different chemical and corundum turns into some of the most beautiful gems in the world, such as red ruby, blue sapphire, and star sapphire.

Corundum crystals are always six-sided. They come in three shapes—barrels, tablets, and spindles (as shown).

A sapphire to a jeweler is a gem made blue by the mineral almenite. To a geologist, any corundum gem that's not a ruby is a sapphire—whatever its color!

Ruby is such a useful material, because it is so hard, that now most rubies are made artificially. Experts can easily tell synthetic rubies from natural rubies, though.

Corundum, being the second-hardest mineral after diamond, is often used as an abrasive for sanding surfaces smooth. It is also used to give extra grip on skateboards. The corundum used may be synthetic, or from a rock called emery.

Spinel

Spinel is a group of oxide minerals, the best known of which is the gem also called spinel. Gem spinel can be red, green, or turquoise. It forms in metamorphic rocks such as marble and gneiss, and in pegmatites.

> ▶▶ **TYPE**: oxide
> **HABIT**: eight- or twelve-sided box-shaped crystals
> **COLOR**: typically red, but also green to black
> **LUSTER**: vitreous (glassy)
> **STREAK**: white
> **HARDNESS**: 7.5-8   **SG**: 3.6-4

Chromite

Traces of chromium are found in many minerals, including emerald, and it gives them their color. But only chromite contains enough chromium to be useful as an ore. It's mostly found in dark igneous rocks such as peridotite.

> ◀◀ **TYPE**: oxide
> **HABIT**: grainy masses
> **COLOR**: black, dark brown
> **LUSTER**: metallic
> **STREAK**: brown
> **HARDNESS**: 5.5   **SG**: 4.1-5.1

Rock Star!

Many famo[us] "rubies" in royal jewels are really spinels!

Chrysoberyl

One of the hardest gems, chrysoberyl gets its name because it looks like beryl but is typically gold-colored ("chryso" is Greek for "gold"). It forms in pegmatite dikes and mica schists, or where granites meet mica schists.

> ▶▶ **TYPE**: oxide
> **HABIT**: typically long prism-shaped crystals, often twinned
> **COLOR**: yellow, green, yellow-green
> **LUSTER**: vitreous (glassy)
> **STREAK**: white
> **HARDNESS**: 8.5   **SG**: 3.7

LOOK

prism-shaped crystals

Hematite

Just as your blood gets its color from the iron it contains, the iron in hematite turns rock and soil blood red ("haimatitis" is Greek for "blood red"). Hematite is a key ore of iron, and it forms as kidney-shaped lumps, flower-like clusters of flat crystals known as iron roses, and earthy masses called red ocher.

TYPE: oxide
HABIT: earthy masses or kidney shapes
COLOR: steel-gray to red in earthy forms
LUSTER: metallic to dull in earthy forms
STREAK: red
HARDNESS: 5.6 **SG**: 5.3

Hematite in the **dust on Mars** helps make the planet glow red!

Nice Nugget!

Perovskite

Perovskite is the world's most abundant mineral, but most of it lies deep in Earth's mantle and it is rare on the surface. It is an ore of the very strong, light metal titanium.

TYPE: oxide
HABIT: box-shaped crystals
COLOR: dark gray, brown
LUSTER: submetallic, waxy
STREAK: white to gray
HARDNESS: 5.5 **SG**: 4

Rutile

Reddish rutile is a key ore of the metal titanium. It's famously found in Switzerland in pockets called vugs. It also forms needle-shaped crystals, and sometimes needle-like strands inside gems such as sapphire.

Rutile strands

TYPE: oxide
HABIT: needles and eight-side prisms
COLOR: reddish brown
LUSTER: adamantine (diamond-like)
STREAK: brown
HARDNESS: 6-6.5 **SG**: 4.2

119

Cassiterite

Cassiterite is the main source of tin. Its hard, black, pyramid-shaped crystals are found in granite and pegmatites, and in skarns near granite. But most cassiterite occurs as grains washed into river gravel—the best source is from old riverbeds under the sea off Southeast Asia.

TYPE: oxide
HABIT: pyramid- or prism-shaped crystals, grains
COLOR: black or reddish brown
LUSTER: adamantine (diamond-like) or greasy
STREAK: white, brownish
HARDNESS: 6-7 **SG**: 6.6-7

LOOK

dark, prismatic crystals

Ultra-shiny crystals

Q. What did one magnet say to another?

Franklinite

Franklinite has a similar chemical make-up to magnetite, and it's also magnetic. But franklinite's magnetism is so weak that this an easy way to tell them apart. It is found only in the famous Franklin mine in New Jersey and in nearby Sterling Hill.

TYPE: oxide
HABIT: typically large eight-sided crystals
COLOR: black
LUSTER: metallic
STREAK: brownish-black to reddish-brown
HARDNESS: 5.5-6.5 **SG**: 5.1

Magnetite

This is one of the few naturally magnetic minerals. Its magnetism and its very dark color and black streak make it easy to identify. Magnetite is a key ore of iron. It's found in igneous rocks and in sands formed from them.

TYPE: oxide
HABIT: usually masses or grains
COLOR: black
LUSTER: metallic to dull
STREAK: black
HARDNESS: 5.5-6.6 **SG**: 5.1

A. I find you very attractive!

Cuprite

This common ore of copper forms when other copper minerals are exposed to the air. That's why you often find it near the surface of rocks in earthy lumps. A red earthy mass covered in bright green is very likely to be cuprite.

▲ **TYPE**: oxide
HABIT: earthy masses or eight-sided crystals
COLOR: deep red
LUSTER: adamantine (diamond-like) to dull
STREAK: brick red
HARDNESS: 3.5-4 **SG**: 6

Gibbsite

A key ore of aluminum, gibbsite is one of the main ingredients of the earthy rock bauxite. It forms under tropical forests where rocks rich in aluminum are weathered in the steamy conditions. You can recognize it by its strong clay smell.

▲ **TYPE**: hydroxide
HABIT: typically massive, breaking into plates
COLOR: white or colorless with colored edges
LUSTER: vitreous (glassy) to dull, pearly when cracked
STREAK: white
HARDNESS: 2.5-3.5 **SG**: 2.4

Brucite

Brucite forms when magnesium-rich minerals such as olivine and periclase are altered by hot, watery fluids. It's common near chlorite and talc schists.

▶▶ **TYPE**: hydroxide
HABIT: typically plates or fibers
COLOR: white or colorless with colored tinges
LUSTER: vitreous (glassy), or waxy and pearly when cracked
STREAK: white
HARDNESS: 2.5-3.5 **SG**: 2.4

Dig It!

Brucite is so soft a mineral that you can scrape off the white masses of plates with a fingernail.

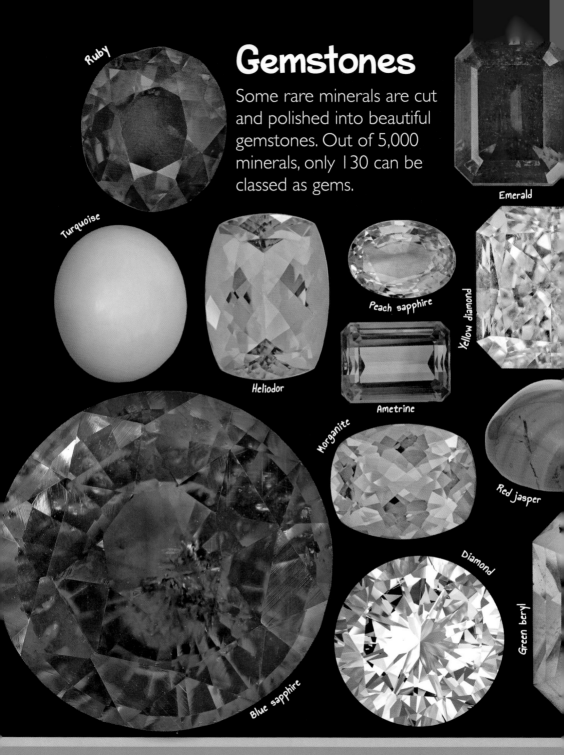

Ruby

Gemstones

Some rare minerals are cut and polished into beautiful gemstones. Out of 5,000 minerals, only 130 can be classed as gems.

Emerald

Turquoise

Peach sapphire

Yellow diamond

Heliodor

Ametrine

Morganite

Red jasper

Diamond

Green beryl

Blue sapphire

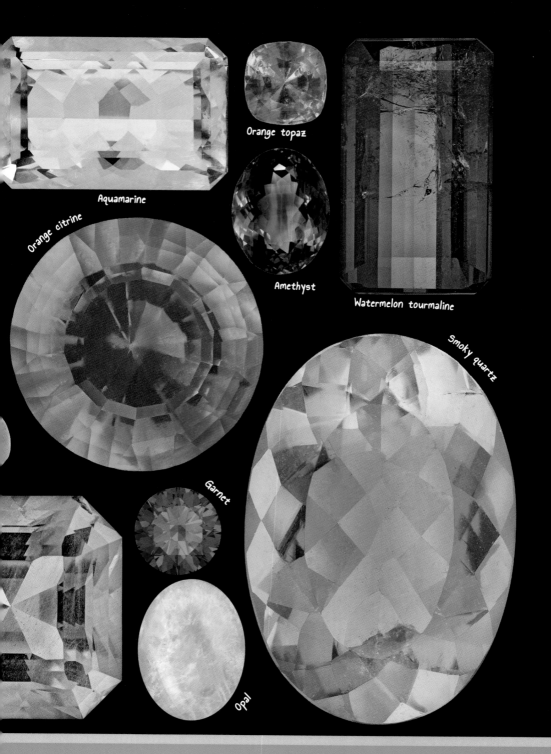

Orange topaz

Aquamarine

Orange citrine

Amethyst

Watermelon tourmaline

Smoky quartz

Garnet

Opal

Halides

Halide minerals form when a metal joins with one of the halogen elements fluorine, chlorine, bromine, or iodine. Sometimes called salts, they include halite—the salt on your fries.

▼ TYPE: halide
HABIT: typically cubes or eight-sided crystals
COLOR: any
LUSTER: vitreous (glassy)
STREAK: white
HARDNESS: 4 SG: 3-3.3

Fluorite

Fluorite comes in more colors than any other mineral. It's typically purple, but it can be just about any other color too. Even a single crystal can be multicolored. Fluorite glows in UV light brilliantly because it contains traces of uranium.

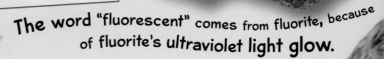

The word "fluorescent" comes from fluorite, because of fluorite's ultraviolet light glow.

Nice Nugget!

Sylvite

Sylvite is similar to halite, but it is potassium chloride, not sodium chloride. It is the world's principal source of potash, which is used to make fertilizers. Crystals of sylvite and halite look similar, but sylvite crystals have cut-off corners. With masses, you can identify halite because it powders if you cut it—sylvite doesn't.

◄◄ TYPE: halide
HABIT: mostly masses, but sometimes box-like crystals
COLOR: colorless or white tinged red
LUSTER: vitreous (glassy)
STREAK: white
HARDNESS: 2 SG: 2

Halite

Halite is also known as rock salt and it's used to make the salt added to your food. It is mined from thick underground beds that formed long ago, when oceans evaporated in very hot conditions.

▶▶ **TYPE**: halide
HABIT: mainly masses, or cubic or hopper crystals
COLOR: clear or white, pale blue or pink
LUSTER: vitreous (glassy)
STREAK: white
HARDNESS: 2 **SG**: 2.1

▼ **TYPE**: halide
HABIT: needle-like crystals and coatings
COLOR: dark green
LUSTER: vitreous (glassy)
STREAK: light green
HARDNESS: 3-3.5
SG: 3.75

Dig It!

Salty inland lakes, like the Great Salt Lake in Utah and the Dead Sea between Jordan and Israel, are good sources of halite.

Atacamite

Green gives the game away that this is a copper mineral, copper chloride. It forms only in very dry conditions, when other copper minerals are exposed to the air. It gets its name from one of the world's driest places, the Atacama Desert in Chile.

Rock Star!

Before blotting paper was invented, people used moisture-thirsty atacamite to dry out messy ink blots.

Sulfides & sulfosalts

Sulfides are heavy, shiny minerals in which sulfur joins with one or two metals with some spectacular results! Sulfosalts are rare variations involving a semi-metal such as bismuth.

Galena

You can easily identify galena by its box-shaped, gray metallic crystals. It is rich in lead and is also a key source of silver. It forms in veins of hot fluid along with pyrite, sphalerite, and chalcopyrite.

Nice Nugget! Cinnabar was once crushed to make the red **paint vermilion.**

Cinnabar

Bright, blood-red cinnabar gets its name from the Persian for "dragon's blood." Cinnabar forms from hot fluids either in veins near the surface or around hot springs. It is the main ore of the metal mercury.

▶▶ **TYPE**: sulfide
HABIT: masses, needles, diamond-shaped crystals
COLOR: red
LUSTER: adamantine (diamond-like) to metallic
STREAK: red
HARDNESS: 2-2.5 **SG**: 8.1

LOOK

boxy crystals

lead gray

▲ **TYPE**: sulfide
HABIT: cubic crystals
COLOR: dark silvery gray
LUSTER: metallic to dull
STREAK: lead gray
HARDNESS: 2.5 **SG**: 7.5-7.6

Chalcopyrite

Chalcopyrite is sometimes called "peacock copper" because it tarnishes to a shimmering rainbow of colors—greens, blues, and purples. It forms in veins and pegmatites and is the world's main source of copper. It's typically made of tiny, yellowish, pyramid-shaped crystals.

Covellite

Covellite is a stunning, glimmering indigo blue color. It turns purple when wet and may tarnish black or deep purple. It forms by the alteration of other copper minerals in veins.

Dig It!

The best covellite crystals occur at Butte, Montana, once known as the "richest hill on Earth" due to its mining reserves.

🔺 **TYPE**: sulfide
HABIT: masses or pyramid-shaped crystals
COLOR: yellow, with turqoise tarnish
LUSTER: metallic
STREAK: dark green
HARDNESS: 3.5-4 **SG**: 4.2

🔺 **TYPE**: sulfide
HABIT: plate-like hexagonal crystals and sheets
COLOR: shimmering indigo
LUSTER: metallic
STREAK: gray to black
HARDNESS: 1.5-2 **SG**: 4.6-4.8

Bornite

Bornite tarnishes to a greeny purple like chalcopyrite, so it's often called "peacock copper" too. The tarnish is oxides of copper. Scrape away the tarnish, though, and you'll see it's pink. This is how to tell it from chalcopyrite.

🔺 **TYPE**: sulfide
HABIT: usually masses, or tiny crystals
COLOR: pink, with turquoise tarnish
LUSTER: metallic
STREAK: gray to black
HARDNESS: 3 **SG**: 4.9-5.3

Orpiment

The yellow of orpiment says "DO NOT TOUCH!" This mineral is poisonous because it contains arsenic, and its garlic smell is a giveaway. It forms, together with realgar, in veins and volcanic outlets.

▲ **TYPE**: sulfide
HABIT: flakes or pillared masses and crusts
COLOR: yellow
LUSTER: resinous to pearly
STREAK: yellow
HARDNESS: 1.5-2 **SG**: 3.5

Millerite

Millerite is known for its amazingly long, hair-thin crystals, which grow criss-cross in cavities in limestone. It can also form crusts and grainy masses and is an important ore of nickel.

▶▶ **TYPE**: sulfide
HABIT: sprays of needles
COLOR: brassy yellow
LUSTER: metallic
STREAK: greenish black
HARDNESS: 3-3.5 **SG**: 5.3-5.5

 Millerite is often found in meteorites— that's out of this world!

Nice Nugget!

▶▶ **TYPE**: sulfide
HABIT: varied, often cubic crystals
COLOR: brassy yellow
LUSTER: metallic
STREAK: greenish black
HARDNESS: 6-6.5
SG: 5.1

Bismuthinite

Bismuthinite is a key ore of the rare native element bismuth. It develops a slightly yellow shimmering tarnish when exposed to the air. It forms where bismuth is altered by hot fluids in veins and in pegmatites.

▶▶ **TYPE**: sulfide
HABIT: fibrous masses or sprays of needles
COLOR: steel gray to white
LUSTER: metallic
STREAK: gray
HARDNESS: 2
SG: 6.7-7.2

Dig It!

Pyrite gives out a spark if you hit it with a hammer. That's how you know it's not real gold!

Arsenopyrite

Like pyrite, arsenopyrite can resemble gold. But unlike pyrite, do not touch, this mineral is TOXIC. Hitting it would release the telltale garlic odor of deadly arsenic. It's often found where nickel silver and tin are mined.

Realgar

As with orpiment, with which it is often found, realgar's telltale garlic odor shows it contains POISONOUS arsenic. Use its deep orange or blood-red color as a warning. The red decays to orange and specimens crumble if they are exposed to the air for long.

🔺 **TYPE**: sulfide
HABIT: wedge-shaped crystals, often twinned
COLOR: brassy white-gray, tarnishes pinky brown
LUSTER: metallic
STREAK: dark gray to black
HARDNESS: 5.5-6 **SG**: 6.1

🔺 **TYPE**: sulfide
HABIT: flakes or pillared masses and crusts
COLOR: orange to red
LUSTER: resinous to adamantine (diamond-like)
STREAK: yellow
HARDNESS: 1.5-2 **SG**: 3.5

Pyrite

This shiny iron mineral can look so much like gold that it's sometimes called "fool's gold." But you can tell it's pyrite if it has cubic, grooved crystals—or if it shows signs of rust! Pyrite gets its name from the Greek for "fire."

Mineral masterpieces

Nature has created some seriously spectacular mineral formations around the world. If you ever get the chance, go and see them!

The cones are mostly made of silicates.

Fly Geyser

As hot water spouts from deep underground at Fly Geyser, Nevada, it deposits tall cones of minerals. The cones become covered in algae, turning them into magical, rainbow-colored mounds.

Fly Geyser, Nevada

IT'S AMAZING!
Kelimutu volcano on the Indonesian island of Flores has three different-colored lakes, turned blue, red, and green by minerals.

Fabulous formations

From sky-blue pools in snow-white terraces to menacing sulfur-yellow landscapes, here are some of Earth's most jaw-dropping, eye-popping mineral deposits.

At Pamukkale, Turkey, hot springs carrying carbonate-rich water bubble up to the surface. The water deposits a gel that crystallizes into calcite minerals, forming brilliant white terraces of the rock travertine.

Salar de Uyuni in Bolivia is the world's largest salt lake. High in the Andes Mountains, water has evaporated to leave a vast level area of halite—salt. This salt lake contains two-thirds of all the world's lithium.

Scan the horizon at Danakil, Ethiopia, and you feel like you're on another planet! It is superhot and contains geysers and volcanic vents that create strange sulfur deposits and giant crystals of olivine and pyroxene.

New Zealand's Moeraki boulders are not aliens' eggs but mineral balls known as septarian concretions, made from cemented mud with veins of calcite and quartz.

Marcasite

Marcasite can look like pyrite, another iron sulfide, but marcasite crystals are blade-like, not blocky. It also changes color and crumbles when exposed to the air. It forms near the surface in places where acidic fluids, including rain, trickle down through limestone, shale, and clay.

◀ **TYPE**: sulfide
HABIT: bladed crystals or massive
COLOR: pale yellow
LUSTER: metallic
STREAK: greenish brown
HARDNESS: 6-6.5 **SG**: 4.8

Nice Nugget!

Marcasite is reflective and was used for mirrors in ancient times.

▶ **TYPE**: sulfide
HABIT: crust or powdery coating
COLOR: dark gray to black
LUSTER: metallic
STREAK: shiny black to gray
HARDNESS: 2.5-3 **SG**: 5.5-5.8

Acanthite

Acanthite is a great mineral to find, since it's 87 percent silver! Surprisingly, acanthite looks shiny gray-black rather than silver. It gets its name from the Greek world "akantha," meaning "thorn," because of its spiky masses.

Chalcocite

Chalcocite is up to 80 percent copper by weight and is found together with other copper sulfide minerals such as covellite and chalcopyrite. It's not easy to distinguish between them, but chalcocite tends to be darker in color.

▲ **TYPE**: sulfide
HABIT: branching
COLOR: shiny gray to black
LUSTER: metallic
STREAK: shiny black
HARDNESS: 2-2.5 **SG**: 7.2-7.4

Sphalerite

Sphalerite is the main ore of zinc. It gets its name from the Greek word "sphaleros," meaning "treacherous," because it's easy to mistake it for other minerals!

Dig It!

A US penny is 97.5% zinc and 2.5% copper. The price of zinc has risen so much that it costs more than one cent to make a penny!

TYPE: sulfide
HABIT: blocky crystals or grainy masses
COLOR: dark brown
LUSTER: adamantine (diamond-like), resinous
STREAK: buff
HARDNESS: 3.5-4   **SG**: 4.0

LOOK

sprays of needles

Stibnite

Often found in veins with quartz or around hot springs, stibnite is prized by collectors for the amazing sprays of needle-like crystals it sometimes creates. Stibnite is the main source of the metal antimony, which is used to add strength to lead and tin.

TYPE: sulfide
HABIT: sprays of needles
COLOR: steel gray, silver
LUSTER: metallic
STREAK: dark gray
HARDNESS: 2
SG: 4.5-4.6

Tetrahedrite

This mineral is named after its distinctive crystals, which form gray tetrahedra (triangular pyramids). It usually occurs as masses rather than crystals. It's quite rare, but it's rich enough in copper to be used as an ore sometimes.

▶▶ **TYPE**: sulfide
HABIT: masses, or pyramid crystals
COLOR: gray
LUSTER: metallic
STREAK: black brown
HARDNESS: 3.5-4 **SG**: 5

Nice Nugget!

Ancient Egypt's famous Sphinx is made from a

Tennantite

Tennantite is an ore of copper, with traces of arsenic that mean it produces a harder metal than pure copper. Some experts believe that tennantite was the source of some of the first copper used by humans thousands of years ago.

▶▶ **TYPE**: sulfide
HABIT: massive or chunky little crystals
COLOR: flint gray
LUSTER: metallic
STREAK: reddish gray
HARDNESS: 3-4.5 **SG**: 4.7

LOOK
small chunky crystals

Pyrargyrite

Pyrargyrite is rich in silver. Its name comes from the Greek "pyr" meaning "fire" and "argyros" meaning "silver." Pyrargyrite turns dark if exposed to the air, but you can wash off the tarnish with soap and water.

▶▶ **TYPE**: sulfide
HABIT: prism crystals, or masses
COLOR: dark red, tarnishing black
LUSTER: adamantine (diamond-like)
STREAK: purplish red
HARDNESS: 2.5 **SG**: 5.8

Sulfates, chromates, molybdenates, & tungstates

When a metal combines with oxygen and either sulfur, chrome, molybdenum, or tungsten, these minerals are formed.

...type of gypsum called alabaster.

Gypsum

Gypsum, the shape-shifter, has many different forms. It typically occurs in thick, soft, white beds where salty water evaporates. This form of gypsum is used to make plaster for covering walls in houses. Other forms are fiber-like crystals or crystals of selenite.

Wulfenite

Crystals of wulfenite are flat and almost transparent, and they often lock together in clusters. They're mostly yellow, but brilliant orange crystals have been found in the Red Cloud Mine, Arizona.

Scheelite

Scheelite is the US's main source of the super-tough metal tungsten, although most of the world's supply comes from wolframite. Collectors love scheelite for its double pyramid crystals and its vivid blue-white fluorescent glow in UV light.

Rock Star!
Tough, heat-resistant tungsten is used on the outside of rockets and in the filaments of lightbulbs.

Barite

Barite is seriously weighty for a nonmetal mineral, and its name comes from the Greek word "barys," meaning "heavy." It occurs along with quartz and fluorite in veins formed by hot fluids.

TYPE: sulfate
HABIT: many varieties
COLOR: white, off-white
LUSTER: vitreous (glassy) to pearly
STREAK: white
HARDNESS: 2 **SG**: 2.3

Anglesite

Anglesite gets its name from the Welsh island of Anglesey, where the Romans went to look for it, for its lead content, almost 2,000 years ago. Today the best crystals come from Tsumeb in Namibia and Toussit in Morocco.

TYPE: sulfate
HABIT: massive or chunky little crystals
COLOR: colorless, sometimes yellow
LUSTER: adamantine (diamond-like)
STREAK: white
HARDNESS: 2.5-3 **SG**: 6.4

Brochantite

You can tell brochantite is a copper mineral from its vivid green color. It's often found together with other greenish copper minerals such as malachite, azurite, and chrysocolla. You can see it forming on bronze statues when they corrode.

TYPE: sulfate
HABIT: prisms, needles, and coatings
COLOR: emerald-green, black
LUSTER: adamantine (diamond-like)
STREAK: pale green
HARDNESS: 3.5-4 **SG**: 4

Dig It!

The best way to see brochantite is to go to a museum and look at ancient bronze statues. The green corrosion is brochantite.

Chalcanthite

Collectors love chalcanthite for its rare crystals, colored vivid blue by copper. The crystals form only in super-dry areas. This mineral soaks up moisture so quickly that it soon falls apart. It must be kept in airtight containers!

> ▶ **TYPE**: sulfate
> **HABIT**: stalactitic masses or crusts, rarely prism-shaped crystals
> **COLOR**: blue
> **LUSTER**: vitreous (glassy)
> **STREAK**: white
> **HARDNESS**: 2.5 **SG**: 2.1-2.3

LOOK

short, prismatic crystals

vivid blue

Crocoite is named for the crocus flower that gives us the orange-yellow spice saffron.

Nice nugget!

Crocoite

Crocoite crystals are some of the brightest and most beautiful. This fragile mineral gets the orangeish color of its splinter-like crystals from the metal chromium.

> ▼ **TYPE**: chromate
> **HABIT**: splinter-like clusters
> **COLOR**: orange-red
> **LUSTER**: adamantine (diamond-like) to greasy
> **STREAK**: orange-yellow
> **HARDNESS**: 3.5-4 **SG**: 6

More minerals

The non-silicates are a mixed group that differ widely in their chemistry. Though far less numerous than silicates, they come in just as amazing an array of colors and forms.

Pyrrhotite (sulfide)

Adamite (arsenate)

Anhydrite (sulfate)

Bauxite (hydroxide)

Pyrolusite (oxide)

Rosasite (carbonate)

Hilgardite (borate)

Sperrylite (sulfide)

Atacamite (halide)

Mimetite (phosphate)

Bournonite (sulfosalt)

Celestite (sulfate)

Wolframite (tungstate)

Apatite (phosphate)

Aurichalcite (carbonate)

Organics

Gems made from plants and animals and their products are known as organics. Ancient peoples used them for jewelry, as they are softer than mineral gems and easier to shape. Coal is also organic, although it is actually a type of rock.

Coal

Coal is the only rock that burns. It is made from the remains of plants that died and were buried hundreds of millions of years ago. The deeper and longer it is buried, the richer and darker it becomes. The deepest, blackest coals are anthracites.

Anthracite

TYPE: organic rock
COLOR: black
TEXTURE: earthy to crystalline
MAIN MINERALS: carbon and organic minerals
HOW FORMED: by alteration of organic matter

Rock Star!

Coal-fired power plants produce about 41 percent of the world's electricity!

Spotlight on coal

Coal is made primarily of carbon. The journey from plant to coal is known as carbonization.

Around 360 mya, dead plant matter gathers at the bottom of swamps and bogs. It decays slowly.

Plant matter is buried over thousands of years. It rots into a dark, compact mud known as peat. Carbonization begins.

As peat is buried deeper, the pressure squeezes water out and concentrates the carbon, forming a soft, brown sedimentary coal called lignite.

The lignite turns into harder bituminous coal sometime between 100 and 300 mya. This type of coal burns quickly.

Eventually bituminous coal becomes anthracite. It is metamorphic rock because of the high pressures and temperatures it has endured. It burns slowly, so makes a very efficient fuel.

Coal mines

Coal is often buried deep underground. The only way to mine it is to cut huge networks of rooms and tunnels into the deep coal seams. Coal mining can be dangerous work.

Coal is eventually compressed into a thick layer called a seam. The thickness of a coal seam can range from just a few inches to hundreds of yards.

Shell

Many mollusks build up their shells with a hard brown protein called conchiolin. They then line it with a beautiful, shiny material called nacre (also called mother-of-pearl), which is made from alternating layers of conchiolin and the mineral aragonite.

Copal

Like amber, copal is solidified tree resin, usually found in the tropics. But while amber is usually at least 10 million years old, copal is much younger—just a few thousand years —and soft and paler in color. It is often crumbly and can be burned as incense.

▶▶ **TYPE**: organic
HABIT: alternating layers of conchiolin and aragonite
COLOR: rainbow pearly white
LUSTER: pearly
STREAK: white
HARDNESS: 3.5-4 **SG** 2.9-3

▶▶ **TYPE**: organic
HABIT: nodules and droplets
COLOR: coffee
LUSTER: resinous
STREAK: white
HARDNESS: 2 **SG** 1.1

Pearl

Pearls form when an irritatant such as grit gets in an oyster's shell. The oyster secretes layers of nacre around the grit and builds up a beautiful shiny ball. The biggest pearls come from sea oysters, but freshwater mollusks also make pearls.

▲ **TYPE**: organic
HABIT: alternating layers of conchiolin and aragonite
COLOR: rainbow pearly white
LUSTER: pearly
STREAK: white
HARDNESS: 3.5-4 **SG** 2.9-3

Rock Star!

When amber solidified, it trapped lot of bugs in it, helping us to identify over 1,000 extinct species!

Coral

Coral is the cup-shaped skeletons, or "corallites," of tiny anemone-like sea creatures called polyps. The polyps take dissolved calcite from the water and turn it into aragonite to make their corallites. A reef is made up of millions of corallites.

Don't Dig It!

Coral reefs are dying all over the world because of overfishing and pollution. Coral is to be looked at, not taken away.

▶▶ **TYPE**: organic
HABIT: tiny cups fused together
COLOR: pink
LUSTER: dull or vitreous (glassy)
STREAK: white
HARDNESS: 2-2.5 **SG** 1.1-1.3

Amber

Amber looks like a gem. In fact it is a resin that oozed out of trees millions of years ago, then turned solid. It is usually found in dense, wet sediments, such as clay and sand, that formed in lagoons and on riverbeds long ago—especially around the Baltic Sea in northern Europe.

◀◀ **TYPE**: organic
HABIT: nodules and droplets
COLOR: amber (yellow orange)
LUSTER: resinous
STREAK: white
HARDNESS: 2 **SG** 1.1

Jet

Jet is a shiny, black organic material that comes from trees that lived long ago. Like coal, it is made of carbon, but while coal is compressed where it fell, jet was made from logs that floated out to sea and sank to the seabed.

▲ **TYPE**: organic
HABIT: lumps
COLOR: black
LUSTER: vitreous (glassy)
STREAK: white
HARDNESS: 3-4 **SG** 12.6

Fossil finding

Discovering a fossil is one of the great thrills of collecting. Fossils give us a glimpse into life on Earth millions of years ago. They also help geologists to compare and date rocks.

Wall of Bones

Most people think of dinosaurs when they think of fossils. The Wall of Bones at the Dinosaur National Monument in Utah contains over 1,500 dinosaur fossils still embedded in it!

Fantastic fossils

Fossils are remains of living things preserved in stone. They are nature's works of art and also windows into the past showing how life has changed. Fossils provide key insights into the history of the rocks you find them in.

The fossil is eventually exposed on the surface when surrounding rock is worn away.

Fossil formation

Fossils take millions of years to form. They usually only preserve the hard parts of animals—shells, teeth, or bones. The fossils may look like the original, but they actually are usually replicas. Most fossils are shellfish that lived in shallow seas.

1. The shellfish dies, falls to the sea floor, and is buried in mud.

2. As the shell is buried deeper, it dissolves to leave a mold.

3. Chemicals crystallize in the mold to form a perfect replica.

4. The mud turns to rock, encasing the fossilized shell.

Imprint fossils are made when remains are squeezed so hard that they are preserved as imprints in the rock, a bit like the way you press flowers.

Index fossils

Geologists look for "index fossils." These are fossils that are widespread but lived only at a particular time in Earth's history. If they spot an index fossil in a rock, the geologists can identify and date the rock at once.

The same index fossil appearing in two separate rock layers shows the layers are the same age.

Trace fossils

It's not just body parts that make fossils. Any signs that animals leave behind—tracks, burrows, eggs, poop—can be preserved, too. They're known as "trace" fossils.

This huge dino print was found in Thailand. Gulp!

These fossilized eggs are from a dinosaur. Fossil eggs are mostly solid stone, but on rare occasions the embryo inside the egg may be fossilized as well.

Scientists call fossilized poop "coprolites." The picture shows the poop of a sea creature called an ichthyosaur, which lived at the time of dinosaurs.

Finding the footprints of dinosaurs preserved where they stepped in mud is not just exciting—it also tells scientists how these awesome animals walked.

Plants

Plants were the first living things on land. They appeared on Earth many millions of years ago. Plant fossils are unusual because their soft tissues rarely formed clear fossils.

Nice Nugget!

In 2012, a 298-million-year-old forest was found in a cave in Mongolia, preserved in volcanic ash!

Seed-ferns

Growing between about 420 and 150 mya, seed-ferns were the first plants to make seeds. They looked like today's ferns, although modern ferns reproduce by spores, not seeds.

Horsetails

Horsetails are plants that still grow today. But 300 mya, they grew to the size of trees, and it is their remains that help to form coal. Horsetail fossils have a bamboo-like pattern on their trunks.

Dig It!

One of the best places to find fossils is in the spoil heaps from old coal mines.

Club mosses

Like the horsetails, today's tiny club mosses had huge ancestors. Around 300 mya there were club mosses that resembled big palm trees. You can spot club moss fossils by the mottled pattern of their trunks.

Simple sea creatures

The first simple creatures appeared in the oceans, and a few left behind fossils. They include some of the oldest fossils ever found.

Bryozoans

Almost microscopic in size, bryzoans form colonies. When fossilized, these colonies can look like lace on rock. Bryzoans are among the most common fossils. Over 15,000 different bryzoan species have been found in fossils.

Sponges

Sponges are simple and very ancient animals, dating back to Precambrian times (over 540 mya). Most sponge fossils formed more recently, though, such as in the Cretaceous Period (around 100 mya).

Graptolites

Graptolites were tiny, worm-like creatures that left billions of distinctive black fossils on dark shales. They date from about 540 to 318 mya. Each era had a different type of graptolite, so graptolite fossils can be used to date rocks.

LÓOK

graptolite fossils

Mollusks & brachiopods

The most common of all fossils, shellfish, such as mollusks and brachiopods, have been around for about 540 million years. They are found in nearly all sedimentary rocks.

Ammonites

Ammonites are beautiful fossils of mollusks with a spiral shell. They're also geologists' favorites: not only are they common, but they also show such clear changes over time that geologists can use them to date the rocks they're found in.

Gastropods

Gastropods are creatures like snails, slugs, conchs, whelks, and limpets. They are most common in rocks that are around 250 mya. Their spiral shells are often preserved as fossils.

Cracking up! Q. What's the most mischievous fossil? had turned to stone.

Belemnoids

Now extinct, belemnoids were squid-like creatures with a distinctive shell shaped like a bullet. They are common in rocks that date back 200–100 million years.

Brachiopods

Brachiopods are also called lampshells, because their shells are shaped like ancient Roman lamps. Their fossils are common in ancient sedimentary rocks from 250 to 540 mya.

The spiral shell housed the ammonite's soft, tentacled, squid-like body.

Medieval people thought ammonites were snakes that St. Patrick

Nautiloids

Nautiloids were the first cephalopods—animals like octopuses and squid. Nautiloids had beautiful round shells. They are common in rocks between 488 and 200 million years old.

A. A nautiloid!

Bivalves

Although bivalves have been around for over 500 million years, their fossils are especially common in sedimentary rocks formed over the last 250 million years—from the age of the dinosaurs to more recent times.

Arthropods
& other small creatures

We know a lot about invertebrates, including insects and sea creatures like crabs and lobsters, that lived millions of years ago, because they were captured as fossils.

Trilobites

Trilobites look like a cross between a crab and a woodlouse. They crawled over warm ocean floors. What's preserved in fossils is their amazing segmented exoskeleton. They died out about 250 mya.

Dig It!

The best place to find trilobite fossils is on a beach near shale cliffs.

Crack ing up!

Q. Why didn't the trilobite move?

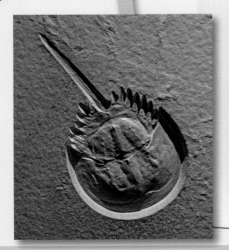

Chelicerata

The rugged chelicerata were like armored tanks that patrolled the floor of prehistoric oceans. These creatures, looking very like today's horseshoe crabs, first appeared about 488 mya.

Insects

Insects appeared soon after the first arthropods made it onto land, about 400 mya, and they quickly took over. Giant insects, such as dragonflies with wingspans of up to 28 in (70 cm), ruled the swamps 300 mya.

Insects trapped in amber may be preserved perfectly.

Myriapods

Myriapods were like the centipedes and millipedes of today. They had legs on each of their body segments. Myriapods were the first land animals. Without competition, they grew to huge sizes—some were over 6 ft (2 m) long!

Echinoids

Echinoids are marine creatures, like sea urchins and starfish, that have round bodies. Complete echinoid "tests" (body casings) are rarely preserved well as fossils. Most sea urchin remains are found in rocks from the last 140 million years.

LOOK

for a whole round urchin

body pattern repeats five times

A. It needed fossil fuel!

...osaurs & other vertebrates

...f vertebrates (animals with
...nes) are super-exciting finds,
...'re rare because skeletons
...rly always crushed by rocks.

...aurs

...etons are
...hard to
...y about
...od ones
...r been
...ed! Head to
...akota's Badlands
...ance of success.

Triceratops
had a beak
like a bird.

This paleontologist (fossil
scientist) is removing a dino
bone from the plaster casing that
it was sealed in for safe transport.

IT'S AMAZING!
In 2016, scientists in Argentina found a huge femur (thigh bone) of a dinosaur. The bone was an incredible 8 ft (2.4 m) long!

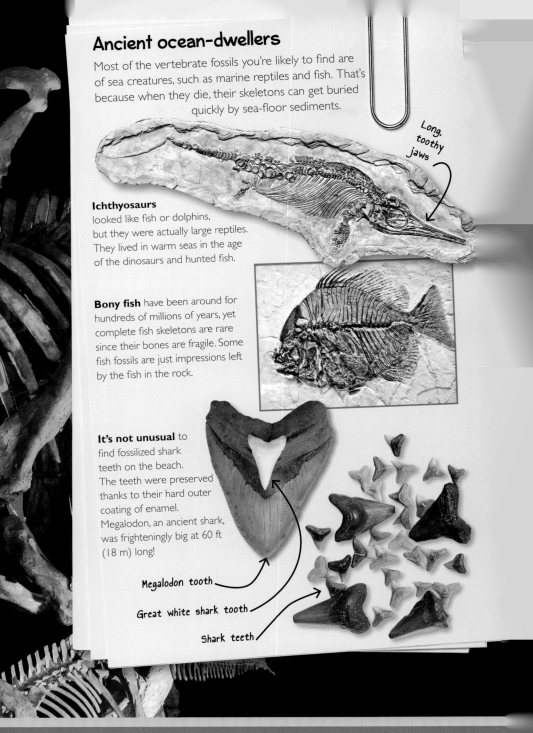

Ancient ocean-dwellers

Most of the vertebrate fossils you're likely to find are of sea creatures, such as marine reptiles and fish. That's because when they die, their skeletons can get buried quickly by sea-floor sediments.

Long, toothy jaws

Ichthyosaurs looked like fish or dolphins, but they were actually large reptiles. They lived in warm seas in the age of the dinosaurs and hunted fish.

Bony fish have been around for hundreds of millions of years, yet complete fish skeletons are rare since their bones are fragile. Some fish fossils are just impressions left by the fish in the rock.

It's not unusual to find fossilized shark teeth on the beach. The teeth were preserved thanks to their hard outer coating of enamel. Megalodon, an ancient shark, was frighteningly big at 60 ft (18 m) long!

Megalodon tooth

Great white shark tooth

Shark teeth

Glossary

Dioptase

adamantine With a sparkling luster like diamond.

arthropod A creature with an external skeleton or case and many legs, such as an insect or spider.

atom The basic part of an element. Crystals are made up of repeating units of atoms, arranged in regular patterns.

batholith A huge, lumpy dome-like intrusion of magma underground that forms coarse-to medium-grained igneous rock.

botryoidal Shaped like a bunch of grapes.

calcite A mineral form of the chemical calcium carbonate. It is in living things as bone and shell and in many rocks, including limestone and marble.

clastic rock A sedimentary rock built up from broken fragments of other rocks.

clint The block in a limestone pavement.

concretion A rounded mass of minerals that grows from dissolved minerals in sedimentary rock.

conglomerate Sedimentary rock formed from pebbles cemented together.

contact metamorphism When rock is altered locally by direct contact with hot magma.

crust The outermost layer of a planet or a hardened layer, coating, or deposit on the surface of a rock.

crystal A basic geometrically shaped, often clear solid that forms minerals. It's built by the knitting together of atoms into a framework. The shape of the crystal depends on how the atoms knit together.

crystallize To form crystals. Can occur when water evaporates from minerals or if the temperature changes.

dendritic Having a branching, treelike structure.

deposit An amount of rock or mineral that has accumulated naturally in one place.

diagenesis The process by which sediments turn to stone.

dike A sheet of rock formed in a fracture within a body of preexisting rock.

dissolve When a solid material breaks down and becomes mixed with a liquid.

element A substance that cannot be broken down into simpler ingredients.

evaporite Rock formed from the dissolved minerals left behind as solids when water evaporates.

extrusive igneous rock Igneous rock formed when lava and other volcanic material that has erupted on the Earth's surface cools.

fluorescence A glow of color when viewed in ultraviolet light.

foliated With thin, leaflike layers that can be split apart.

fossil The remains of an animal or plant from the past, preserved in stone.

fracture The chipping or breaking of a stone in a way unconnected to its atomic structure.

geode A usually small cavity in a rock, with crystals lining the inner surface and growing toward the center of the geode.

grike A crack in a limestone pavement.

hydrothermal Relating to water heated underground, often erupting in hot springs or geysers.

hypabyssal Relating to intrusive igneous rock that forms only a little way underground.

igneous rock Rock that forms from magma. The molten magma rises from Earth's hot interior then cools and solidifies as it nears the surface or erupts.

inclusion Something inside a mineral crystal such as a gas pocket, or an internal crack, or a needle of another mineral.

intrusive igneous rock A body of igneous rock that invades older rock.

iridescence A rainbowlike display caused by the way light plays off features just below the surface of the material.

lava Molten rock that erupts at Earth's surface. Lava is called magma when it is still underground.

lopolith A large, saucer-shaped intrusion of igneous rock.

luster The particular way mineral reflects light.

magma Molten rock that can crystallize underground or erupt at Earth's surface as lava.

massive Relating to a mineral made up of a shapeless mass with no visible crystals or grains.

matrix The mass of finer grains in which larger grains or crystals are embedded.

metamorphic rock Rock made by the alteration of other rocks under extreme heat and pressure.

metasomatism Metamorphism by a chemical change where a rock interacts with a liquid.

microcrystalline Having crystals too small to see except under a microscope.

native element A mineral made from just a single, naturally occurring element, such as gold.

nodule A small, irregularly rounded mass or lump of a rock, mineral, or mineral aggregate.

nugget A small lump of gold or other precious metal.

nummulitic Containing the shells and other debris of prehistoric sea creatures.

oolitic Consisting of tiny balls made from layers of calcite.

opalescence A milky blue form of iridescence.

opaque Impenetrable by light; the opposite of transparent.

ore A metal-rich mineral or rock that can be mined for a profit.

pegmatite A formation of rock created when magma cools into veins and cracks in the aftermath of a volcanic eruption.

phenocryst A large crystal set into the matrix of an igneous rock.

plutonic Intrusive igneous rock that solidified from magma deep underground.

prism A solid with ends of similar and equal shape that are parallel, or a solid with triangular sides joining at a point

pyroclastic Made up of old solidified magma blasted out in bits by an erupting volcano.

regional metamorphism Metamorphism that takes place on a large scale deep beneath mountains as plates shift.

resin A yellow or brown substance obtained from the gum or sap of some trees.

Fluorite

sediment Material, such as silt, sand, or gravel, transported and deposited by water, ice, or wind.

sedimentary rock Rock made from sediment.

sill A sheet of rock formed between, and parallel to, existing layers of rock.

specific gravity A measure of how dense a mineral is compared to water.

stalactite A spike of carbonate minerals that grows down from the roof of a cave.

stalagmite A spike of carbonate minerals that grows up from the floor of a cave.

streak The color of a mineral when it is scraped over a white, unglazed ceramic tile.

tarnish To dull the luster of a surface.

transparent See-through, clear, or crystalline.

twinned crystals A pair of mineral crystals that grow together.

vein A thin sheet of minerals that fills a crack or fracture in a rock.

vesicle A small cavity in volcanic rock that was formed by gas trapped inside the lava.

vitreous With a glasslike shine.

Pyrite

Index

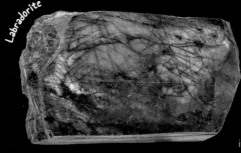

Labradorite

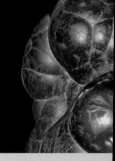

Emerald

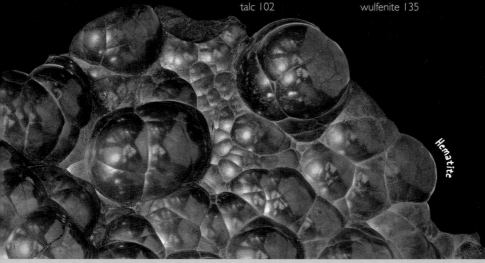

Hematite

Credits

Photos ©: Alamy Images: back cover Amethyst (BENJAMIN PENNANT), 144, 145 (Chris Howes/Wild Places Photography), 38, 39 background (Doug Perrine), 16 bottom left (geoz), 55 center top (Michael Grant Travel), 16 background, 17 background (Peter Cripps), back cover Dolomite (PjrStudio), back cover Lapis Lazuli (Renata Pavlickova), 78 top right, 86 bottom right, 87 bottom left (Shawn Hempel), 59 top left (Siim Sepp), back cover center top geode, 153 top right (The Natural History Museum), back cover Fluorite (Valery Voennyy); David Iliff: 40-41 background; Dreamstime: 19 paintbrush (Aaphotographer), 139 top right (Álvaro Ruiz Tintoré), 19 toothbrush (Borys Shevchuk), 100 bottom left (Branko Jovanovic), 19 chisel (Charles Rausin), 81 center left blue stone, 82 center left, 139 bottom center (Daniel127001), 143 top (Dave Bredeson), 24 top right (Derrick Neill), 142 bottom right (Erika Kavali), 126 bottom left (Fabrizio Troiani), 39 center right (Farbled), 149 top right (Flowertime), 38 center left bottom (Fokinol), 138 center right top Howard Sandler), 19 safety hat (Hywit Dimyadi), 127 bottom right (Infinityphotostudio), 117 center right top Ingemar Magnusson), 141 center (Jan Gottwald), 83 center left (Jiri Vaclavek), 142 top left (Ken Backer), 53 center (Likrista82), 107 center right top (Marcel Clemens), 122 center right bottom (Martin Novak), 51 bottom left (Matthew Mcclure), 142 bottom left Michael Kempf), 32 top right (Michal Baranski), 19 trowel (Onur Ersin), 117 center right bottom Photographieundmehr), 80 bottom center (Sergey Lavrentev), 139 center left (Tatiana Morozova), 118 center left (Tilzit), 19 magnifying glass (Vladislav Gajic), 18 top right (VvoeVale), 82 top (Willi Van Boven), 31 center left (Yuriy Chaban), 97 bottom right (Zbynek Burival); Fotolia: 11 top left (Andreas Wass), 81 bottom right (diamondtetra), 32-33 background (Elmo Photo), 81 center right center bottom (imfotograf), 85 center Jiggo_Putter), 24-23 bottom stones, 125 top right jonnysek), 85 bottom (Krzysztof Wiktor), 9 center right top (Leonid Andronov), 73 top left (lunamarina), 121 bottom (marcel), 8 bottom left map (nataliya_rodenko), 104 top right (niki), 157 top right (photoworld), 134 bottom left, 139 center top (PIXATERRA), 57 bottom left siimsepp), 43 bottom center (Tyler Boyes), 34 bottom left rock, 119 bottom left, 128 bottom left, 138 center left top (vvoe), 15 notepad and throughout (windu); Stockphoto: 33 center right bottom (35007), 2 top left, 108 top left, 141 center bottom (A_Pobedimskiy), 110 bottom right, 134 top (aeduard), 15 notepad image 7 AlbertPego), 117 bottom center (AleksandarNakic), 81 top center right (Alphotographic), 140-141 background andresr), 36-37 cracks and throughout (AndSim), 53 top (Anita_Bonita), 30-31 background (anthonyspencer), 19 bottom right (ArgenLant), 98 top left, 154 bottom left screen (benedek), 41 center right top (bigapple), 15 notepad image 3 (Billybrant310), 16-17 top (borchee), 1 top right (Brian Adducci), 22 center left, 82 center right, 155 bottom right (BruceBlock), 73 center left carolo7), 81 top left (chapin31), 131 center left (choja), 81 bottom center right (cl2004lhy), 76 bottom center screen (cobalt), 55 top center (code6d), 33 top right Cylonphoto), 23 bottom right (Dafinchi), 17 center left DanielPrudek), 97 top right (Dash_med), 60-61 background (DavidStorm), 15 top left screen (demarfa), 5 center bottom (demerzel21), 147 bottom left dgero), 22-23 background (didecs), 94 center left

(DIYA3), 22 bottom left (EriksvoBoda), 105 bottom left (Estellez), 24-23 background (fcafotodigital), 25 bottom right screen (FinnBrandt), 28-29 background (Fodor90), 20-21 background (fotoVoyager), 15 notepad image 2 (Furchin), 126 center right (g-miner), 33 center right top vineyard (goag), 15 notepad image 5 (GoodLifeStudio), 131 center bottom (GoodOlga), 25 top left and throughout (Grafner), 22 bottom center (grauy), 61 center top (Guenter Guni), 9 top right (hadynyah), 94 bottom left, 108 bottom right, 109 bottom left, 149 top left, 150 center left, 150 bottom center, 151 bottom right, 152 center (hsvrs), 11 center right top (HTOUDY), 33 center right top grapes (Hyrma), 90-91 background (iluziaa), 2 left background (ithinsky), 35 center right eyes (JakeOlimb), 23 center right (JoKMedia), 53 bottom left, 53 bottom center (jollyphoto), 83 center right hand and throughout (karelnoppe), 152 bottom left (kellymarken), 93 bottom right (Kerrick), 23 top right (krichie), 15 notepad image 6 (Lady-Photo), 81 top right (Leamus), 21 top left (Linda Steward), 81 top far right (lore), 41 center left (lucentius), 11 top right (MagicDreamer), 115 top right, 115 bottom right, 125 bottom, 132 top, 137 bottom right, 146-147 background (MarcelC), 54-55 background (Marclschauer), 155 bottom left (Mark Kostich), 61 center bottom (Meinzahn), 95 top right (merial), 137 top right (michal812), 152 bottom right, 153 bottom left (mizikm), 40 bottom left screen (Moorefam), 41 bottom right magnifying glass (mrgao), 11 center right bottom (MundusImages), 95 bottom right (MVorobiev), 102 top (nastya81), 39 center left (NNehring), 141 top right (Oktay Ortakcioglu), 15 top left camera (Pablo631), 81 center right center top (papa1266), 19 paper background and throughout (Paperkites), 17 top right (PaulMorton), 14-15 background (Pavliha), 141 center top (Perytskyy), 46-47 background (PHILMACDPHOTOGRAPHY), 17 bottom right hand and throughout (photka), 35 top left paper and throughout (Picsfive), 33 top left, 34 top left paper and throughout, 35 bottom right paper and throughout (poplasen), 151 top right (qingwa), 81 bottom center left, 120 center (raiwa), 77 top right (Reimphoto), 82 center (rep0rter), 41 center right bottom (Romko_chuk), 122 bottom left top (royaltystockphoto), 123 bottom center top (Rozaliya), 47 center right (rsiel), 77 top center left (rusm), 58 bottom left (sakdinon), 26-27, 131 center top (sara_winter), 18-19 background (Saturated), 148 bottom left (scigelova), 70 top far right rock (sergeichekman), 21 bottom (stevanovicigor), 33 bottom right (stockcam), 123 bottom center bottom (SunChan), 61 top (SurkovDimitri), 52-53 background (swedewah), 67 top right (Terryfic3D), 19 rock pick (tiero), 65 top left (tilzit), 8 bottom left hand and throughout (Tolga TEZCAN), 80 top right hand and throughout (Tom Merton), 14 top left (TPopova), 15 notepad image 4 (Turnervisual), 131 top center (tverkhovinets), 131 bottom (UpdogDesigns), 47 top right (ventdusud), 155 center (Violetastock), 141 bottom center (Vitalina), 99 bottom left, 140 bottom left (VvoeVale), 15 notepad image 1 (wabeno), 150 center right, 151 center left (wakila), 24 center left (Watcha), 25 top center (wdstock), 16 center right (WendyOlsenPhotography), 146 bottom left screen (Wicki58), 12-13 (WLDavies), 123 center top (YolandaVanNiekerk), 8-9 (Yuri_Arcurs), 46 bottom left screen (zhangguifu); National Geographic Creative/Carsten Peter, Speleoresearch & Films: 74, 75; NERC/BGS Groundhog/NERC 2017: 20 center; NOAA/OAR/National Undersea Research Program (NURP): 39 bottom left (Peter Radcliffe: 22-23 tray, 30 bottom screen; Science Source: 17 bottom right screen (Alan Sirulnikoff), 124 bottom left

hes B. Winter), 19 bottom (De Agostini/Dagli Orti), 41 bottom right rock (De Agostini/A. Rizzi), 96 background, 97 background (Diccon Alexander), back cover center top Smithsonite, 89 top right, 121 top left (Dirk Wiersma), 87 center (E. R. Degginger), 20 bottom (Gary Hincks), 9 center right bottom (Georg Gerster), 65 bottom right, 69 center left, 89 bottom right, 94 bottom right, 101 bottom right, 111 top right, 112 top left, 112 bottom, 117 top right, 118 bottom right, 128 top right, 132 bottom, 134 bottom right (Harry Taylor/Dorling Kindersley), 62 top right, 70 bottom right, 72 bottom left (Joel Arem), 72 bottom center, 73 center right bottom, 73 bottom right (Joyce Photographics), back cover bottom center, 83 bottom left, 106 bottom left screen, 106 bottom right screen (Mark A. Schneider), 67 center bottom (Mark Williamson), 25 top right (Peter Bowater), 136 center left (Phil Degginger/Jack Clark Collection), 120 bottom left (Science Stock Photography), 57 top left, 71 bottom left, 98 top right (Ted Kinsman); Shutterstock: 66 bottom left screen (Action Sports Photography), 97 center right (AGCuesta), 154-155 background (AKKHARAT JARUSILAWONG), 103 center right (al_1033), 53 bottom right, 80 center left, 91 center right bottom, 100 bottom right, 108 top right, 108 bottom left, 109 center right, 111 center left, 111 bottom right (Albert Russ), 99 bottom right, 100 top left (Branko Jovanovic), 9 bottom right (Catmando), 148 top right (CoffeeChocolates), 100 top right (Coldmoon Photoproject), 11 bottom left (elenaburn), 11 bottom right (Fedorov Oleksiy), 48 bottom left, 58 center right (Fokin Oleg), 155 top (frantic00), 101 top left (Jiri Vaclavek), 14 center (JPL Designs), cover, back cover top background and throughout (Juli Hansen), 39 center right (kavring), 141 bottom right (Lee Prince), 81 top far left (LesPalenik), 11 center left (Linett), 91 bottom right (Madlen), 138 bottom left (MarcelClemens), 130-131 background (Michael Flick), 43 top, 149 bottom (michal812), back cover fossilized fern (Mirka Moksha), 1 bottom (MrBright), 147 bottom right (netsuthep), back cover magnifying glass and throughout (new photo), 107 center right bottom (Oreena), 62 top left (papa1266), 81 top center left (Ryan Tanguilan), 148 bottom right (Sementer), 66-67 background (turtix), 31 top, 34 top left rock, 48 top right, 49 top right, 56 center (Tyler Boyes), 10 top (upsidesmile), 10 bottom, 25 center right, 34 bottom right, 35 bottom left, 62 bottom left, 65 top right, 102 bottom left, 102 bottom right (vvoe), 34 top right, 42 bottom right, 44 center right, 47 center left, 63 top left, 85 top left (www.sandatlas.org); The Open University: 77 top left; USGS: 110 top left (Carlin Green), 115 bottom left; Wikimedia: 127 top right, 138 top left, 142 top right (Didier Descouens), 143 center right (Geni), 49 center right (Keith Pomakis/Canadian Museum of Nature), 72 bottom right (Mark A. Wilson/Dept. of Geology, The College of Wooster), 35 center rock (Mikenorton), 57 center (Pterre), 88 center bottom, 121 top right, 132 center (Rob Lavinsky, iRocks.com), 107 top right (Vassil).

All other images © Scholastic Inc.

The publisher would like to thank the following people for their help:

Penny Arlon, Neal Cobourne, John Farndon, John Goldsmid, Tory Gordon-Harris, Shari Joffe, Marybeth Kavanagh, Ed Kasche, Debbie Kurosz, Rachel Phillipson, Steve Setford, Ali Scrivens, and Bryn Walls.

Calcite